I0475572

Men on the Inside:

Observations of Deviance: Thirteen Prison Character Types

First Printing: 2015

ISBN 978-1-365-30790-4

Blackamoor Publishing

16252 Prince Drive

 South Holland IL, 60473

www.blackamoorpublishing.com

Table of Contents

Foreword

Men – and women – end up in prison for various reasons, some because of their own malfeasance, and many through a turn of events beyond their control. As the disparity in material wealth and opportunity in the American populace increases, more stringent measures are imposed to perpetuate the advantage of those in power. Those presuming to represent 'the law' act more and more not to find reasonable solutions, but to reinforce their power and presumed authority, specious as it may be. The net effect is that police – and courts – operate to sustain the appearance that they are 'doing something' against crime, criminalizing more issues, and especially using the war on drugs to make themselves look good. With mandatory sentencing, and 97% of all arraignments going to plea bargains where the prosecutor – with no public accountability – fills the roles of accuser, judge, jury and sentencer, US prisons hold many who are no threat at all to society, while hardened and wily menaces to human well-being continue to roam free. The US now incarcerates more prisoners than any other nation in the world, both proportionally and in absolute numbers, an all too painful illustration of the ancient observation: the more laws, the more criminals.

With the increase of 'privatization', the courts and those who own stock in the private corporations have a strong financial incentive to maintain a steady flow of subjects into prison. Indeed, contracts between prison for profit corporations and the government stipulate explicitly that the state the government will maintain 90% occupancy of private prison facilities. Privatization only means that tax revenues are applied not to support prisons owned and operated by the state, but to prisons operated by corporations and their stockholders.

Beholden to profit seeking stockholders, prisoner operators cut costs wherever possible, reducing food quality and guard pay, failing to provide advertised programs supporting rehabilitation and reentry, while augmenting revenues through additional expenses on the imprisoned and their families with 'gotcha' commissary, telephone and other fees. Prison is a profitable industry; it has nothing to do with reformation and rehabilitation of human beings or the health of society.

The exploitive practices of the private prison industry and those feeding into it of themselves erase any clear distinction between 'criminals' and 'normal people'. The reality is that there is no clear distinction between the good guys and the bad guys. All human beings have the same spectrum of needs, and are capable of the same repertoire of feelings and behaviors. It is a fallacy to believe that there is a clear distinction between 'criminals' and 'normal' people on the outside, despite the operating premise of prisons that those convicted are 'not OK', while presumably those who do the convicting are 'OK'. Life in any circumstances has its stressors. Incarceration is stressful; beyond the loss of freedom, deliberate practices within the prison system, and by those who run it, generate additional stress.

No one is immune from stress. Stress causes deviance from a state of balance. Deviate behavior is a coping mechanism taken to an extreme, a set of desperate measures to return to balance or a state of comfort, anything to alleviate deep pain. All human beings, indeed all living creatures, respond of necessity to stress, some in obvious ways, others not so clearly evident. Men on the Inside: Observations of Deviance is a study of thirteen-character types or patterns observed over more than fifteen years of incarceration.

-KL

Preface

In 1993, I was the director of security for New Life Self-Development, a security company owned by my then father-in-law Leonard Farrakhan Muhammad[1]. Our company was contracted by the Chicago Housing Authority (CHA) to provide security for several public housing buildings, those being: Rockwell Garden Apartments, Ogden Court Apartments, and Maplewood Courts.

As an unarmed security company, our primary function was to secure the lobbies, upper floors, inside grounds, and perimeter. Since we were unarmed our authority afforded us no more than the power to detain. On the occasions where an arrest was warranted, our post required us to contact the CHA Police or the Chicago Police who were assigned to respond to our call.[2]

Beside security, New Life took on the additional challenges in community outreach and conflict resolution; they were my secondary duty alongside being the director. Conflict resolution was my most daunting task as director. It involved direct intervention in the affairs of rival gang members who harbored age-old grievances and drug territorial disputes. It was an effort I took great pride in mediating.

---

1. Leonard Farrakhan Muhammad was the Chief of Staff and son-in-law for the Nation of Islam leader Minister Louis Farrakhan. I married Leonard's daughter Denise Farrakhan Muhammad in 1996. We divorced after my incarceration.
2. As one of the biggest housing developments in the country, Chicago Housing Authority (CHA) had its own police department called CHA Police. Due to CHA's sheer size and rampant criminal activity, it would have been virtually impossible for the Chicago police to respond to crime throughout the Chicago metropolis as well as the Chicago Housing developments. CHA police received plenty of criticism and drew hundreds of law suits but with the random violence and isolated dysfunction I couldn't imagine what those housing developments would look like without the CHA police presence.

When we first arrived as the new security personnel, Rockwell Gardens' living environment was so infested with gang and drug activities that the life chance for law abiding citizens was virtually impossible. With the amount of structural deviance[3] pushing up against us on every side, we were immediately thrust into a war zone filled with dangers and perils even armed guards before us were incapable of overcoming.

I recall performing the very first security walk-through of Rockwell when I noticed boys from ages 8-16 hanging out with the unruliest individuals I have ever seen. Coming from my background, that's saying an awful lot. Instantly I surmised that we had to provide these boys with better models of manhood to emulate, because what I saw in them was a germ of my past which grew more familiar with each boy's hand I shook. Every building we entered had its own deviant characteristic, equipped with the stench of urine from one end of the hallway to the next. Just when I thought things couldn't get any worse, what we encountered next would leave an indelible stain on my psyche. To this day I still find myself cringing at the thought of what my virgin eyes bore witness to.

While making rounds on the upper floors along with two other officers; a duty I required all New Life guards to perform every 45 minutes to an hour, we stumbled upon a female drug addict in her mid to late forties performing oral sex in the stairwell on a 15-year-old drug dealer in exchange for crack cocaine. Walking up on this act of sexual impropriety threw me back on my heels in shock. Don't get me wrong, I'm no moralist. It's not as if I've never seen fellatio being performed on someone before, especially since adolescence has a way of exposing our eyes

---

3. Structural Deviance is a term I use to describe behaviors prevalent in public housing and prison structures where the lack of resources cause segments of that community to break laws in order to acquire goods and services, more so in prison houses than anywhere else.

to things our minds aren't prepared to engage in with informed observation.

When I was a deviant teenager I would "sneak-a-peek" at my uncles' porn collection and on occasion catch a glimpse of the adult programs on the pay-per-view programs of my day known as "Spectrum or On-TV", you know the things little mannish boys do for kicks. Therefore, I was no stranger to what I encountered in the stairwell. My discomfort and shock were due to my Islamic conversion and therefore moral ideation to respect, protect and honor women as Allah would have me to honor mothers, wives and sisters. So, my shock was a direct result of these ideals I believe in.

As the kid dealer began pulling up his pants to gather himself, my shock and awe developed into shame and disappointment. Feeling a need to give the teenager a lecture on his unchecked impropriety of playing "Russian roulette" with the HIV virus, for five minutes I engaged the kid about the dangers of his actions. But hearing none of my self-righteous preaching, the female crack addict began to express her concerns about the need of her $10 for performing the sexual act. Furthermore, she believed and adamantly expressed the fact that her not being able to complete the job wasn't her fault and how she in fact had earned the ten dollars the l5 year old kid promised her. Lost on her was the understanding that her act amounted to statutory rape. For me to continue imparting values in the head of this kid I had to eliminate his being distracted by the female addict so I directed him to pay the lady as he promised so we could continue our conversation. He complied, and paid.

I would have liked to do more for the lady in the stairwell but her substance dependence wouldn't allow me to reach her at that moment. So, for me, the most pressing issue was save the kid[4]. I must say my encounter with this kid proved to be

---

meaningful, one which allowed me to gauge our purpose for working at Rockwell in the first place. As a socially responsible company I knew we had to devise a plan to properly engage and outright challenge Rockwell's decades of gangs, drugs and violence, I had to figure out a way to win the residents' trust. So, we devised several approaches to achieve this end:

I. We met with the tenant president and staff of each building (8 in all). We discussed new Life Security objectives to reduce crime and violence, along with our goal to create a more livable environment to raise their children in peace. I listened to their suggestions, concerns, and views on how to best achieve our security objectives.

2. I knocked on the doors of over a thousand apartments to introduce myself as head of security. Each tenant was given my business card to call me in the event of a problem or concern.

Note: If New Life was to be successful, I understood early on the need to develop a relationship with the occupying residents. They needed to see me as their ally for change because the deviant criminal element we had to go up against were their boy-friends, husbands and sons.

---

[4] Whether in Rockwell Gardens or the ghetto of Watts, the scourge of crack cocaine in a poor environment is demoralizing, thus rendering caretakers, women, vulnerable to performing acts so despicable they are no longer recognizable. Her ability to be rational in matters of righteous living has been completely hijacked by a euphoric desire she will forever pursue until she comes to a crossroad of total recovery or eternal flat-line. No matter the time, day or year, substance dependency makes slaves of users in every generation. During my days of youthful deviance, I regretfully bore witness to a female addict performing a sex act with a dog for the entertainment of a bunch of foul teenagers in exchange for a ten-dollar bag of crack. Encountering that kid in the hallway with the female addict brought me back to those days. But more than anything, walking up on such foulness made me reflect on the power drugs have over humans: that a 40 something woman was powerless to help herself or the kid she was essentially molesting, thereby placing them both at risk. This is a universal story where economically deprived individuals find solvency and escape in a bag of dope. Make no mistake about it, these acts are economic just as well as spiritual.

3. We created the Rockwell Junior Tenant Patrol. This approach was my way of establishing a relationship with the children of the tenants in hopes to reduce their desire to do drugs or to commit senseless crimes. Rockwell Junior Tenant Patrol was responsible for picking up paper and debris in and around the buildings. When the elevators broke down the Jr. Patrol helped the elderly tenants carry grocery bags up the stairwell to their apartments.

4. To solidify my relationship with the tenants I moved my family into the building with the worst gang and drug activity.

Note: I must say this was a scary move for me; one which put the fear of God in my wife. After a lot of negotiating with my wife I could convince her to support my efforts to change the living conditions at Rockwell.

5. The last approach was to establish communication with the gang elements in all 8 buildings.

Note: This was the most difficult task of all since the gangs had long perceived our mission as a security company was to disrupt drug sales and the deviant activity (which exacerbated crime) in Rockwell.

Just like we planned, it wasn't long before the children of Rockwell housing project began to view us (New Life personnel) as role model; I reflect on the times my car would pull up to any of the eight buildings, anywhere from l0 to 15 kids would surround my vehicle. When this first happened, I didn't realize the jealousy it induced in the various gang factions.

In hindsight, I realize now my act with the children of Rockwell was an act of war that drastically diminished gang recruitment. Plus, as a security company we provided the kids another model of what manhood looks like without peddling illegal substances. I tell you I was so proud of my boys who sought after change because of our influence.[5]

To our credit, after one year of security detail at Rockwell our efforts created a 90% crime rate reduction and a self-esteem boost for the tenants at large; Just when I thought we were out of the woods and on our way to a systematic change of Rockwell's deviancy, turmoil and violence erupted on every level. In short, gang wars between the Vice Lords and Gangster Disciples broke out on three different occasions. Each time I found myself as chief conflict resolution officer quelling the violence until my security guards became the victims of the very violence we were attempting to quell[6].

---

5. Gang Recruitment – Children don't become gang members on their own without being influenced by those who control the environment they sleep, eat, and play in. It should come as no surprise that the individuals who have the most influence in these communities are not the politicians or religious leaders. This mixture of poverty and hopelessness is the perfect storm for underground economies. Poverty has so taken hold of the children that anything shiny and glittery represents the achievement of the American Dream. Drug dealers know their form of wealth acquisition can lead to death or life in prison, but in super structures like Rockwell being 'dramaturgical' or flamboyant is all that matters. Youth need something to belong to, and gang culture is the most accessible club. Once a youth is intertwined with these urban terrorists, it will take divine intervention to remove this stain. As a culturally conscious company we understood the power of gangs and therefor believed our moral opposition to the residence-lived experience would inspire a desire for change.

6. I am reminded of the meeting Minister Louis Farrakhan had with all the principle people of New Life Security about our purpose for being at Rockwell. He passionately expressed 'if we were not at Rockwell to save our people from their mental and spiritual condition, then we had no business being there'. In fact, Minister Farrakhan was clear about not associating the Nation of Islam with anything that would harm our people. He instructed us (new Life executives) on how to best proceed in this sensitive work of securing and elevating Rockwell's citizens. He threatened to pull the NOI's support from our security company if we didn't go about the business of saving the people which also included saving gang-bangers as well. In hindsight, I surmise Minister Farrakhan understood the moral ineptitude of structures like Rockwell which we sought to transform. I never imagined those things Minister Farrakhan spoke about concerning Rockwell would be the very things responsible for my imprisonment. How could one go from being Savior of the people to Killer? We (New Life Security) should have given more gravity to the Minister's words.

The gun battle between the gang factions got so bad the Traveler Vice Lords in building 2515 unlawfully restrained several of my officers for them to lock down the building they were occupying[7]. They essentially turned building 2515 into an 18-story fortress, locking in tenants and locking out everyone else. After mediating the back and forth shooting from building to building, we were finally able to free my security officers from the horror they were under only to find them beaten up by the Vice Lords.

With the level of tension that developed early on between the CHA Police and our company, it should come as no surprise no arrest was made on our behalf for the action of the gang-bangers against the peace officers. Consequently, they (Traveler Vice Lords) became more emboldened with each action. Soon they began brandishing guns and assaulting our officers on average of once a week. Even still no arrests were made on our behalf. In fact, the CHA police stopped coming around and making rounds in the building altogether. Since no assistance was forthcoming from the Chicago Police and the CHA Police for the assaults, my officers felt their only recourse was to protect themselves and as a result they started to bear arms, including me.

Consequently, the events which lead to my incarceration were brought about soon after peace officer Damon Muhammad was severely beaten by many Vice Lords that left him hospitalized for days and confined to his home for weeks. Officer Damon's

---

7. When we first arrived it was a common occurrence for Vice Lords and Gangster Disciples to shoot at each other from building to building when a dispute broke out. It was no different in this case, but due to the tension between the gang elements and our security they locked our two guards in the building with them. Normally when shootings occurred, the gang members would ask our guards to clear the building to avoid being shot. Hearing about the incident over our two-way radios, I immediately headed to the area of contention and demanded the release of my personnel.

beating was a direct result of responding to a domestic violence dispute on the upper floor of building 2417.[8]

When Damon arrived on the scene, a Traveler gang member named Darvin Harris was physically striking his girlfriend in the hallway. Damon's interference intensified the domestic dispute, angering Darvin who happened to be a ranking member. Words turned into yelling, yelling turned into pushing and shoving. Once the domestic dispute was resolved, Darvin rounded up his gang brothers and proceeded to hunt down Damon to teach him a lesson for having interfered in Traveler's business.

Approximately twenty minutes into their search they spotted Officer Damon behind building 2515 where they proceeded to encircle him to prevent him from escaping. After stating their purpose for engaging him, the men began violently beating the peace officer with bricks, bats, and bottles until his body lay unconscious in the middle of the field. A few minutes later an ambulance was called to extract his body from the scene and rushed to the hospital.

Damon's near-death experience at the hands of Rockwell's gang element had all the security personnel on edge and in fear of their own safety; the type of fear that would cause a young gang member to lose his life and cost me twenty years of my own. As the story goes, three days after officer Damon's assault by the gang element, one of the principal individuals involved in the assault was found dead in the lobby of building 2417.

Several New Life officers were brought in for questioning about the murder but never charged. However, more than four years later, a jail house snitch was offered inducements by the state's attorney's office for testimony that would implicate me in the crime. I was brought to the police station for questioning as to my involvement and charged with the crime of murder. With no evidence and a case built on the hearsay testimony of a

---

jailhouse snitch, I was ultimately sentenced to 40 years in prison. What irony![9]

With nearly 16 years of imprisonment behind me I find myself in the midst of the same deviant characteristics I encountered in the housing complex. Through my observation of the various prison types I'm forced to share my limited space with, it's becoming more apparent that super-structures such as Rockwell Gardens, Henry Horner Homes, and Stateway Garden are and were perfect mechanisms for dysfunction. Like the housing projects (unintentional or by design) prison structures share the same psycho-social dysfunctions since both are havens for the perpetuation of deviancy. Both function in a way that encapsulates the whole 'inmate's self'.[10] The only difference is that one structure acts as subjective housing that

---

8. Peace Office Damon Muhammad who now goes by the name Nuri Muhammad given to him by Minister Farrakhan for his righteous character and unyielding love for the people, currently serves as Head Minister for Mosque # 74 in Indianapolis, Indiana. Damon at the time left Indianapolis to help me and others liberate Rockwell's slums. Unfortunately, the men who ran those projects wanted no part of change and thought our arrival was an affront to the foulness they had come to enjoy. I apologize to Nuri for things not quite working out as we had hoped. Today Nuri (Damon) is one of the foremost Ministers in the NOI. He will do great things in the service of the despised and rejected. I used to think we would be friends and brothers for life; I guess my prison sentence has strained our relationship. I do miss what we had as brothers although my prison experience has given me a new batch of brothers.

9. This particular individual whom I once considered my little brother, for $25 a month and comfortable stay in the county jail lied to the State's Attorney Office about my involvement, in my murder trial.

10. In Erving Goffman's book *Asylum* he uses the term mortification of the Inmate Self to describe how bodies 'are broken by an array of routines and practices'. In society, housing projects break its residents; asylums break its patients, and prison structures break the convicted. All systematically amount to a mortification of the self of the inmate.

confines its residents to demoralizing living conditions in the name of governmental social program. The other subjugates the prisoner's whole being through isolation with routine and rituals while claiming it to be correctional. What's lost on both super-structures is the fact deviant behaviors can thrive while reformative measures aren't given any serious consideration.

However, the subjects of the latter structure (prison) become more deviant due to their apparent proximity. By this I mean that when deviant individuals are placed in an all-encompassing environment of dysfunction alongside other deviant individuals who feed off the same dysfunction, the State unequivocally promotes what I characterize as 'sempiternal malignancy '. Allowing prisoners to go unchecked in environments of sempiternal malignancy renders the whole system of justice to nothing more than passive participants in the ills of the men they ought to be reforming.

In observance of deviance from my vantage point (as a prisoner), I reason that most men occupying these unnatural concrete and steel cubicles are generally good. The daily bombardment of dehumanizing stimuli provides the right ingredients to effectively transform even the most upright and reasonable individuals into the animal these 12x9' cages were constructed to hold.

As a total institution with inherent qualities for debasing the whole 'inmate self', I'm fascinated by the deviant's ability to peacefully exist within an all-encompassing structure of debauchery that endlessly grates against the prisoner's moral resolve.

I likewise reason at the innate quality of goodness to co-exist in peace with 'similar situated other' without the daily eruption of violence. In a structure of limited space and life opportunities, respect and peace are social cornerstones for survival. Make no mistake about it, the total institution of prison is brutal on the psycho-social process of those it encapsulates. The psychological state of each prisoner as he re-enters society is one's rebellion against the prison system. Those who acquiesce to the unnatural setting of prison by suppressing their moral and cognitive ability to rebel against its confines are most likely to succeed. Mind you, to rebel requires discipline and intellectual sophistication most prisoners are mentally inept or too lazy to develop. In rare cases where rebelling against the stultifying intent of prison forms is achieved, such ultra-conscious activity is most often practiced by those prisoners I describe as 'The Radical '(Ch. 9), 'The Prison Hustler (Ch. 10), 'The Jail House Lawyer '(Ch. 11), and the ultimate conscious activity of the 'Intellectual'(Ch. 12).

Unfortunately, with all the observable qualities of goodness that allow prisoners to peacefully exist within their confines often it is the opposite side of truth and goodness which tends to radiate from the core of prison houses. It is this duality of fluctuating seams that Observance of Deviance is intent on displaying.

Prisons for all intensive purpose are erected structures for the housing of societal deviance. It is with this understanding that those responsible for creating prison policies must be held accountable for the human product being reintegrated back into society. Observance of Deviance provides an insider's view on the inefficient nature of the current prison structure to effectively inculcate or cultivate moral and ethical standards for the men who will eventually return to society upon completion of sentence. The 13-character types presented in this book will for better or worse shed light on the irrationality of a criminal justice system void of purposeful and constant reform, while considering the ever-changing landscape of a society encompassing diverse social, political, and cultural ideologies.

We can no longer afford the financial expense of simply warehousing the deviant without sensible policies directed at reforming deviance once it enters prison. I repeat, without the institution of sensible policies that transform the thought process of the men encapsulated by cell walls, prison now and will continue to amount to nothing more than warehouses for social rejects who will eventually be released back into their various communities.[11] If reform measures are not the cornerstone for policy makers, why release ex-felons back into the public unreformed, when research data show that most ex-felons without support will recidivate. Why then aren't we using tax payer dollars more efficiently? Are the issues really that perplexing? Or shall we just be truthful as a society and policymakers about the genocidal – or profit motive – intent of barbed-wires, concrete and steel?

The 13-character types presented in this book are actual real individuals whom I have observed for the past 15 years. Their habits, thoughts, and overall dispositions about people, places, and things should be informing to some and come as no surprise to others. It is my belief that to get the most out of the reading requires one to suspend his/her preconceived notions as to what they think or believe a prison or prisoner is. Likewise, I encourage each reader not to become preoccupied with the foulness of some characters at the expense of judging others. That said, my goal is to show the total institution of prison in its full glory while being as honest and open about the 13-character types encapsulated by her cells.

---

11. Statistics demonstrate that most men who enter prison will eventually return to society.

Introduction

The sound of Joliet's 30-foot gates closing behind our (new prison arrivals) Bluebird transportation bus still sends chills down my spine. How could I allow myself to be placed in such an inferior mess?

As several AR-15 type rifles follow our every movement, the gravity of my offense has now come full circle. Eyes locked in a trance on the rifle wielding guards, my inner voice speaks out: "how could you allow this to happen to us Tyrone? We had so many business opportunities and projects lined up and you threw it all away chasing ideas of friendship and brotherhood that were never real to begin with. Look at you now! Where are your friends and brothers now?"

I have had to live with this self-accusing voice-spirit for nearly two decades, and I believe long after my sentence is over, this voice-spirit will haunt my soul until I'm completely healed from the trauma of confinement. There are so many layers surrounding my incarceration that an autobiography is necessary to flesh out my trials – but that's not what this book is about.

Chapter 1: The Deviant Thug (DT)

"The deviant who is provided no cause to change will eventually revisit his ills on society; it's just a matter of who will be unlucky enough to be his next victim." TFM

Deviant behavior- How does it start?

Deviant thugs tend to come from the most disenfranchised areas of America's inner cities. They are mainly poor blacks, Latinos, and in those rare cases where cultures collide, poor white boys. Most white boys who take on the persona of deviant thug do so because of trying to fit in, rather than as a direct result of poverty and social alienation.

White DTs can blur the lines of social or ethnic class because at least in the abstract their skin color affords them a glimmer of hope of achieving the American Dream.

Although white DTs aren't the subject of this book, they are nonetheless relevant in the overall context of a prison population occupied by thugs and men, because they tend to emulate DT's of color. With prisons composed mainly of blacks and Latinos, emulation of the dominant group is somewhat inevitable, just as it would be for any Black Man attending an all white college. He is bound by his environment to take on characteristics of the dominant group. Thus, distinguishing DTs by their specific cultural origins is not necessary.

Environmental origins of deviant behavior

DTs entering the gates of prison can be classified as having anti-social personality disorder. Anti-social personality disorder is defined in the DSM IV – 'a prevailing pattern of disregard for, and violation of, the rights of others'. This is hard to dispute since nearly every prisoner has been found guilty of violating some social convention, even if such clinical classification doesn't consider the implicit and universal codes which govern the environments occupied by men who would be considered deviant. That is, there is a subculture of individuals within a community who commit acts of violence against one another or what 'street code' would refer to as 'The Opposition'. Because of environmental dysfunctions such as abject poverty, high unemployment rates, broken households, dilapidated schools and dwelling, the DT is in a constant quest for social, political and economic relevance. He feels compelled, in an already marginalized population of men, to fight for both meager resources and personal identity.

It is often within these battles to achieve social, political and financial normalcy (which the media define as the American Dream) that civilians, aka law abiding citizens, get caught in the cross hairs of thugs. This is quite unfortunate given that DTs make up less than 5% of the communities they affect. Nonetheless, DT criminal activity has a terrorizing effect on entire communities and holds them hostage. For DTs, such a pursuit is worth a gamble even if it means life in prison or an untimely demise. 'Get rich or die trying' has become the DT's mantra.

The effect DT's have on the communities they occupy is made even worse because most of these communities are headed by single females; with elderly women playing a pivotal role in rearing small children. Very few professional men and women live in or participate in the community politics of these isolated slums, even though many were born and raised in these areas. In most cases, these professionals still have mothers and other family members relegated to these dysfunctional environments. Therein lays the problem: enclaves of dysfunction are left to be ruled by boys ages 14-25 who ought to be learning themselves how to be good sons, brothers, and men. What we now have is a 14-25 demographic with no guidance or direction improvising fragile manhood concepts and imposing them on an already fragile population. The easy thing would be to cast blame on an unguided mass of youth, solidified by the institution of laws which incarcerate young people with reckless disregard and no consideration for the third world type upbringing seeking to mirror the dominant social order.

This mirroring effect is aided by television, internet, magazines, movies, and music, and bombards young minds with material images: this is the American dream. Then the authorities of society have the gall to pass judgment on disenfranchised youths' preoccupation with procuring things. What kind of madness is this? Are we not to expect those reared in poverty to emulate those controlling 90% of the nation's wealth? Is not opulence and effortless lifestyle presented as the proper way to live? Why then should we be surprised to see desperation and violence emanating from efforts to attain it?

In every corner of America young people observe acts of hypocrisy by so-called responsible policymakers. They are taught early on that through might and violence, peace and wealth are attainable. Consequently, black on black crime and gang activity follow logic like that of governmental policies, even though critics of gangs, drugs, and violence might find cause to disagree with this comparison. In this context, controlling neighborhood blocks for drug distribution justifies violence just as controlling oil producing countries does for America. In either instance power and/or wealth acquisition set the tone for violent behavior. The difference is that the American military conducts war via legislation, while DT's move according to the impulse of their bellies, which inevitably tends to turn out badly.

All such human interactions are driven by similar motivation although they vary morally and ethically, except where authority is given by the people to exercise war for the benefit of the state. Even in this instance the Geneva Convention and other international bodies set parameters through which war is to be executed in a humane way – if ever there is such a thing.

Now let's look at a structure that does more to nurture devious behaviors than it does to foster moral conduct.

The Inherent Structure of Deviousness

When devious youth (ages 17-25) enter prison, they are immediately hurled into three levels of criminal caste. The first level of 'Criminal Pretentiousness' is composed of DT's who are themselves trying to make sense of their prison situation. They are often confused and looking for any familiar face that can help lighten the load through conversation and companionship.

The second level functions from a position I classify as 'Associate Level Deviancy' (ALDs) aka Small Time Crooks (STCs). ALDs are men with criminal convictions ranging from simple drug possession to burglary. This group comes in and out of prison servings sentences between 1-7 years. My observation is that most ALDs commit crimes to satisfy extreme drug habits. As a class of prisoner, ALDs are the shadiest group in character and overall social stratification. It is my assumption their character degeneration seems to stem from a life preoccupied with procuring funds by any means possible to satisfy an addiction to substances.

Since most ALDs never addressed their substance related issues while on the streets, substance dependence characteristics and behaviors follow them to prison. It seems to be a dual issue of substance use and mental illness in most ALD prisoners. But in the humanity of it all, I am convinced more than ever that ALDs and their subsequent recidivism have a direct correlation to mental illness rather than merely a propensity toward criminal activity. For this group, prisons have clearly become makeshift asylums for those suffering from schizophrenia and the like. (See the book: The Protest Psychosis, by psychiatrist Jonathan M Metzl.)

It is therefore unfortunate that correctional facilities are ill-equipped to address mental illness presenting as criminal behavior in the men placed in their charge by the courts. Furthermore, correctional facilities betray the public trust by acting irresponsibly in matters of reform. The public in effect pays several times to keep ALDs as active participants in the prison experience, not to mention the public and private property damage each ALD reaps on citizens in his effort to self-medicate with illicit drugs. The net result is ALD types are the ones bankrupting the criminal justice system. It's not violent criminals – since violent crimes tend to be of an isolated nature.

The third level of deviants occupying prison in significant proportions are 'the Master Criminals' (MCs), aka 500 Level Crooks (5LC's)[12], with convictions ranging from drug conspiracy to murder, with sentences from 8 years to life. Any prisoner serving 8 years or more will without doubt develop master criminal capabilities resulting from interaction with every form of criminal deviancy connected to the prison complex, with one exception being a change of mindset in those prisoners who so choose to tap into higher consciousness by way of creative and synthetic imagination.

In cases where MCs are motivated by higher consciousness, I have affectionately classified these prisoners as: The Radical (Ch 8), The Jail House Lawyer (Ch 10), and The Intellectual (Ch 11). These types are hidden gems in a prison industry concerned only with showcasing the vilest prisoners for political and economic gain. The above prisoners act as counselors, therapists, mentors and guides to other prison types who haven't yet risen above their devious vocation. They are the prison reformers who sadly go unnoticed by the public. Some are left to serve inordinate sentences while others die never having an opportunity to have their self-acquired moral and social transformation recognized.[13] This is an institutional injustice with tragic consequences felt throughout every prison population. DT's who witness this injustice in those prisoners whom they see as morally upright develop doubt regarding change, especially since the above-mentioned prisoners receive no public nor institutional recognition for doing so. Knowing no true reform is forthcoming, DT's have learned to game the system. They come in and out of prison making sure not to commit any violent offense so they can continue

---

12. The description 5LC denotes the level of criminal sophistication, and not necessarily the nature of the crime, nor time and position in gang subculture.

13 As much as legislators are not concerned with the reformation process – which ought to be automatic within any correctional system, the aforementioned character types have painstakingly, without any help from prison officials, sought to elevate their moral and intellectual dimensions. This group, because of their moral and intellectual development, become enemies of a structure which promotes immorality on every level.

receiving good time for doing nothing but sitting in prison planning their next crime upon release.

The exceptional prisoners I mentioned earlier are not afforded an opportunity to good time due to their violent offense, even though morally they have demonstrated their worthiness. More on these exceptional prisoners in the chapters that follow.

In case I have not made myself clear, absolutely all men entering prison are deemed DT's. Over time a select few will find cause to develop higher life aspirations and personal development, except for MCs. The MC finds confirmation and resolve in his permanent criminal status, where prisons in their current bureaucratic formation function as his base of operation. To help the reader grasp how men entering prison as simple DT's often exit as something much more the following scenarios describe how MCs use the current prison structure to foster economic and social autonomy extending well beyond the very structure which ought to render him powerless.

The events in the following scenario are real events, although some details and character names have been changed to preserve prison code of not 'snitching'. I call it 'The Total Institution Scenario of Inevitability'.

The Total Institution Scenario of Inevitability

Ronald: The Deviant Thug   Duke: The Master Criminal
          (DT)   (MC)

Phase 1: Ronald's arrival at Danville CC

As a new face at Danville Correctional Center, Ronald is an instant standout. Within an hour of his arrival he is reunited with many neighborhood homies he long lost touch with due to incarceration. Finding familiar company put him at ease despite the anxiety caused by barbwire and steel obstructions. Since a prison functions with its own folkways, mores and norms, Ronald's apparent nervousness will provide disconnected prisoners a type of CNN view back to the communities they were removed from. For more than hour disconnected men find solace in listening to the ills and joys of Englewood's 16th ward (a crime ridden ward on Chicago's Southside whose citizens live in relative poverty).

Once Ronald fulfills his journalistic duty delivering the neighborhood news, the men extend him the same courtesy by bringing him up to speed on prison rules, code and culture, as well as provide him with the necessary commissary items to give him comfort until he can provide for his own needs. The next 30 to 180 days will bring about Ronald's socialization in to the prison system.

Socialization is an important aspect of acclimatizing to prison life. In prison men separate themselves into classes like society; it's more advantageous to stand unified as a convicted mass against the complex. Prisoners' lack of unity makes serving time that much harder and is a win-win for prison administrators.

Phase 2: Ronald's socialization & Duke's sovereignty

Now fully assimilated into the daily routines at Danville's 'total institution', Ronald finds it easy to make new acquaintances. He possesses what prisoners call an aura of swag, though this isn't so for everyone serving time. Every new prisoner (ALDs and MCs) with whom Ronald develops a bond has a criminal record ten times worse than his own, especially Duke.

MC Duke is serving 60 years for murder and drug conspiracy. When the Judge sentenced Duke he stated, "Society will be a bit cooler now that one of Satan's top helpers has been removed from it." In the Judge's effort to rid society of men like Duke he never factored in the reality that Duke's dynamic personality uniquely positioned him to reign over the very institution in which he was to be punished. Duke's charismatic authority within 4 miles of barbwire and steel fencing serves as the ideal recruiting ground for his continuing criminal enterprise.

Now thoroughly acclimated to institutional life, Ronald's brotherhood of criminality has increased tenfold with Duke as the principal member. Ronald has now begun to take on the DNA (Deviant-Narcissistic-Attitude) of ALDs and MCs in his group.

Phase 3: <u>The bond between Ronald and Duke</u>

Ronald and Duke met during a pick-up game of basketball in the prison gymnasium. As the story goes, after a few arguments over foul calls, Duke took an immediate liking to Ronald because he wouldn't back down. Further inquiry into Ronald's prison stint revealed to Duke that Ronald's time in prison will be short, and therefore ideal to establish a link between him and the world outside his confused reality. Duke sees Ronald as the key to regain his power role in the communities he was removed from. For the next two months prior to Ronald's release date Duke spent more than 8 hours a day grooming him on the lucrative nature of drug distribution. It wasn't long before they became one in thought and principle; the MC Duke has molded an efficient clone of himself. This new-found brotherhood with Ronald is essential to continue his drug empire.

Conclusion

The above scenario is played out each day in prison houses throughout America. As an institution presuming to be structured for correcting a man's ills against man, prisons have nonetheless proven to be no more than havens for unending debauchery and degeneration – an open or tacit I call 'Sempiternal Malignancy'.[14]

Television Programs Watched by Deviant Thugs

- MSNBC
- Lockdown
- Cops

- The Game
- Black Ink
- Bad Girl Club

- Basketball Wives
- WGN

- Bait Car
- First 48
- Jerry Springer
- Maury Povich
- Cartoon Network
- Comedy Central
- Love and Hip-Hop Real Housewives of Atlanta
- Real Housewives of Hollywood
- La La's Full Court Life
- Buckwild
- Honey Boo Boo
- Full Throttle
- Hard Core Porn
- Dog the Bounty Hunter
- Mob Wives
- 106 and Park MTV
- VH1
- News
- Wendy Williams Show
- Ms. America
- Victoria's Secret Fashion Show
- T.I. And Tiny Family Hustle
- Duck Dynasty
- Married to the Game
- FX

Magazines Read by Deviant Thugs

- Jet
- Hip-Hop Weekly
- Vibe
- XXL
- National Enquirer
- Star
- Celebrity Slew
- Ride
- Maxim
- Playboy
- Hustler
- Black Tales
- Big Butt
- Smooth
- Blackmen
- Source
- Video Illustrated

14   Sempiternal Malignancy:

1. Of or pertaining to a perpetual state of deviancy.
2. Characterized by the Master Criminal's ability to pass on criminal habits, behaviors and traits to novice offenders or Deviant Thugs.
3. A convicted prisoner who uses the current structure of corrections (IDOC) as a subculture for his continual criminal enterprise.
4. The capacity of evil to find permanence within an environment devoid of true reformation.
5. One who has accepted immorality and deviancy as an inevitable product of society.
6. A philosophy predicated on the utilization of debauchery and proximity as a tool for obtaining prison debenture.

Chapter 2: Conscientious Thug (CT)

"He who has a why to live for can bear with almost any how."
Friedrich Nietzsche

There's a Method to the Madness

Chapter one describes the basic deviant thug (DT) type, and sets the stage for all characters that follow. The terms used in the proceeding chapters, except for 'The Pervert', 'The Radical', 'The Entrepreneur', and 'The Intellectual', all have compound identities based on the author's observations. For example, personal interaction with prison types unveiled an element of 'Thuggery' rooted in a 'Devious' foundation, hence 'Deviant-Thug'. In developing the definitions and terms for each of these types, three sociological standards were applied.

1) How society view ghettos and prisons

2) How professionals (Psychologist, Sociologist, and Criminologist) views ghettos and prisons

3) How men affected by ghettos and prisons see themselves and the environments which have come to define their self-concept and sociological imaginations.

Applying the above standards allowed as much objectivity as possible. I must confess that at times that objectivity fades as certain emotions show through towards certain prison types who commit crimes against women and children, such as will be detected in chapter 6, 'The Pervert'.

More than Meets the Eye

The Conscientious Thug (CT). On the surface, CT's appear to be no different from their DT counterpart, but a casual conversation reveals a mentality in stark contrast to appearance. As a prisoner who has passed through both DT and CT stage of development, I understand the transformation taking place with CT types as their conduct and search for knowledge was no different from my own.

As far as demographics goes, CTs represent 25% of the prison population. Unlike DTs, CTs straddle the fence between achieving moral excellence and dreams of becoming Chicago's biggest drug dealer. On any given day, you can find CTs in full-throttle gang banger mode and on other days they can be found hanging around prison intellectuals absorbing as much knowledge as a thirsty brain can stand. They love the attention that follows from associating with prison's intellectual class, but as a career thug change proffers a lonely road where fear of criticism acts antithetically to higher learning. Watching CTs navigate stages of growth over 'thuggism' is rather interesting. Their struggle for intellectual fluency is constantly being challenged by environmental stimuli which justify gang affiliation and the like. In his struggle for self-worth the CT begins questioning whether loyalty to street culture is more rewarding than a life regulated by higher principles.

Those on the outside looking in are probably thinking of course, choosing higher principles is better than associating with a bunch of gang banger thugs. Yeah, yeah, yeah, I heard the same critiques when I was a young man engrossed in deviousness, but when all you know how to do is commit bad acts for gain, taking a walk towards right actions is like learning how to swim; ingesting too much water (knowledge) too fast could drown you. Further, the anxiety associated with change can sometimes be unbearable. Luckily for CT's they have a circle of intellectual prisoners to lean on for guidance when difficulty arises – Lord knows no help is forthcoming from prison administrators.

CT: The Interview

Throughout my prison stint I came across many young men fitting the CT description although I never met one more compelling than my former cellmate. He was finding change a difficult process so I encouraged him daily to stick with his search for truth through knowledge, that when he finally found what he was searching for, the struggle would be more fulfilling. I further assured him I would be there whenever he needed to be nudged in the right direction.

As is custom with all prisoners, once trust is established men are then able to let their guards down and open themselves up to real issues affecting their hearts and souls. I shared with my cellmate my plans for writing a book profiling the various criminal forms accompanying prison domains. After that I described to him this CT character type I had formulated and how he as a prisoner striving for changes fit perfectly within the social framework. He agreed with my assessment. We talked for about 15 minutes more before I gathered the nerve to ask if I could conduct an interview about his past and his decision to change. He enthusiastically said yes.

The following interview has been edited for clarity and flow; there were areas I thought were too personal and self-incriminating so they were not included. The interview in its entirety lasted more than an hour.

Q: What's your name?

CT: (deliberately left blank to honor his privacy)

Q: How old are you?

CT: 22. I turn 23 in two weeks.

Q: That's interesting, you're approximately the same age as my son.

CT: Huh, maybe I should start calling you Pops?

Q: Naw, please don't do that; I'm still regretting not being a very good father to my own two children. I'm still learning how to be a good neighbor and a better man.

CT: Cellie, you're too hard on yourself. You one of the better men walking the grounds of prison.

Q: I appreciate your kind words, Cellie, but being great in prison means nothing to my son and daughter whom I abandoned, being great in prison but not great during my time of freedom.

CT: Yeah, I hear you man, I would probably feel the same way if I had kids their age.

Q: Enough about me. Where are you from?

CT: Englewood – Chicago

Q: How long have you been incarcerated?

CT: A little over two years.

Q: So, you came to prison at 19 or 20?

CT: Yes, I was 19 going on 20.

Q: If you care to share, what crime did you commit to be worthy of prison?

CT: With all due respect, Sir, I don't call what I was doing a crime.

Q: (interrupting) you don't have to call me Sir.

CT: Forgive me I don't intend any harm by it; I've been raised to respect my elders and since you are an 'Older Head' (terminology derived from gang culture designating authority or seniority) it is personal choice of mine to show you the utmost respect.

Q: I appreciate it, I'm just not used to being called Sir by a young brother around here. Besides, I'm only 40 (at the time) so it took me by surprise. I'm sorry for interrupting you, please continue.

CT: Like I said, I don't call what I did a crime – but how could trying to feed yourself and your family be considered a crime? In my opinion, a crime was committed against me by removing me from my newborn daughter and baby mother. Who's gonna take care of them now? Surely not the Chicago Police!

Q: Well, young brother I agree the Chicago Police absolutely don't care about who's taking care of your baby daughter while you're behind bars, for that matter neither does the public. But all things being equal what type of rationale justifies committing crime to feed your family when by doing so you essentially cause harm to another family for material gain?

30

CT: Yeah, I hear what you are saying, bruh, I never looked at it like that until just now. But honestly when I was out there in the streets no one cared about me, so I didn't care 'bout nobody. The truth be told I didn't force people to buy drugs from me. I'm a product of capitalism. How is my capitalism different from Americans buying and selling slaves? At least the people who buy my drugs had a choice in whether to buy my product or not, slaves didn't have a choice to be sold or not be sold. You know like I know we don't produce any guns or drugs in Englewood. I should be the one mad. They (the courts and police) took me away from my baby girl for 10 years for some shit (guns and drugs) we don't control or produce[15].

Q: You mentioned ten years? You notice in the beginning of this interview I never asked you about your time or crime because prison code informs that that's a no-no, but since you made mention of it (ten years) express a little more to me how you feel about your sentence.

CT: What the f*%k you want me to say about that shit (appearing visually angered by my questioning)? You should know better than anyone how I feel you doin 40 f*%king years!

Q: OK little homie, I get your point, I feel terrible, but not necessarily about the time I'm serving because I believe in justice. My pain stems from a sense of being trapped within a broken system not inclined toward reform. It's like, at what point do prison administrators and/or policymakers determine whether serving time alone is or isn't an effective mechanism for correcting devious behaviors. My view is prisoners are serving too much time without ever being assessed for moral or ethical aptitude.

Take me for instance, brother, I was ready to be a productive citizen ten years ago but with no process in place to assess social and/or moral competence, hundreds of upright men

---

15 The CT's new consciousness allows him to formulate great concepts of truth although his rationale is often stained by the falsehood justifying his irrationality. His struggle for truth will be one that's long and arduous.

languish in prison 20-30 years; for some prisoners, the correctional system became antithetical towards right conduct. Whom do we blame in this case when prisoners or ex-prisoners lose hope, then proceed to act out, i.e. high recidivism rates? This is my only feeling about serving time little brother, I see it as a systematic state of injustice across the board. Time, I can deal with; I look at it like being in school twenty years. What I don't have tolerance for is injustice and wasting tax dollars in the name of protecting the public from men like us. Which in my opinion some of us (prisoners) are more morally upright than those taking guard over us. So then let me rephrase my question, with the hope my expression has helped to broaden your own. Now that I know how you feel about your ten-year sentence I ask you this, why should society care about you when you seem to justify your criminal behavior against society?

CT: I don't know how to really answer your question, but no I don't expect them (society) to feel what I feel or see what I see because they never walked in my shoes. I never had a father, he was killed when I was a small kid. My mother left me to take care of my sister, chasing cocaine in the streets. I grew up hating my father for getting himself killed and leaving me alone to care for my mom and sister. I didn't have a childhood. My guidance came from street catz; 'cause all I've ever known was the streets and how to survive the best way I could. No one ever came to me and my sister's aid. Now that's some society for your ass, ain't it?

Q: What I'm hearing you say is you pretty much had to become a man at a young age; had to raise your little sister, and that drugs destroyed your mother?

CT: That's right.

Q: So, after seeing all that you've seen why did you start selling drugs to other mothers?

CT: Well, good question. At thirteen or fourteen I had to find a way to put food on the table. I got tired of seeing my little sister go hungry therefore like any brother who loves his sister, I

32

started stealing bread and lunch meat from the neighborhood grocery store. That didn't last long because I got arrested for stealing. When the store owner asked me why I was stealing food – I said because me and my sister was hungry. Can you believe he still called the pigs on me?

Q: Yes, I can.

CT: Anyway, man, my mother had to pick me up from the police station. I knew right then stealing wasn't my thang, I had to figure out something else to do for money. Now one of my classmates worked for a local drug dealer as lookout for the cops; it kept money in his pocket and new shoes on his feet – I wanted in on that. After introducing me to the dealer he worked for I went from lookout man to street dealer in less than three month's time. I recall really loving school but it was no longer more important than being able to feed and clothe my sister. No kid should have to choose food and clothing over education, especially in America. Why did I have to give up my schooling? Why wasn't anyone there for my sister and me? You ask, "why should society care about me now?" because they didn't give uh f*%k about my sister and me then. So, like I said earlier, f*%k society! I am bitter with society; I had to find love, loyalty and food in the streets. I not only lost my education opportunity but ten years of my life as well.

CT, continuing: Now my daughter needs me like my sister before her. F*%k society's criticism of me! (Tears started rolling down his face so I pause the interview to give my cellmate a hug. A kind of Oprah moment. I was surprised he allowed himself to drop his mask long enough to show and receive affection. Five minutes or so elapsed before we continued our interview.)

Q: Boy that was some moment, huh? I can tell you tapped into a time of great pain right there, and I respect you even more for having the courage to show vulnerability. Which brings me to my next question and the logic behind assessing you as a CT character type. Anyone on the outside reading or listening in on this interview would agree that you are indeed conscientious and thuggish. The things we talked about off record further inform me of pride, ego, and unresolved issue masquerading as strength. My question then is, why is it so hard for you to move beyond thuggery to accept principles brought on by higher consciousness? And what will it take for you to do so?

CT: to be honest, I'm scared to death, all I've ever known how to do is gang bang and hustle them streets. From what I see the streets don't respect knowledge, people like yourself don't have the same respect you once had when you ran the streets. People who work every day don't get any respect. People fear and respect power only. Look at all the stuff you do around here for other prisoners, look how positive you are and how you've changed your life; no one even knows that you are here nor do they care. Plus, I fear that if I leave my street dudes I'll be selling them out for change because I can't get them to go with me. That's my problem man! And on top of that who cares if I change or not the world still turns with or without my changing. Prisoners, especially violent prisoners, don't get no good time for change.

Q: Young Brother, you have made many poignant points (he didn't know what poignant meant so I handed him a dictionary) yet I beg to differ with you on two points, one being that no one cares, and the other whether I'm respected now that I'm no longer in the streets. To your first question, if no one cares, why would we be having this conversation?

CT: I'm not talking about you, big homie. I know you care, I'm talking about the people who have power to change prison conditions.

Q: Young brother, we are the people who have the power to change things. Therefore, I'm putting a book like this together on observing prisoners such as yourself, with a prayerful hope that someone with power would read it and begin lobbying for meaningful prison reform that could have a social, political and economic effect on your and my present and future elevation during and after serving our sentence. I might be home by the time this book comes out, but hopefully the prisoners I leave behind will benefit from the reform that could come about because of my book. Prison authority ought to see the practicality of dealing with prisoners in their current mindset and not solely based on past offenses, which in and of itself is un-American and certainly un-Christian. It is our duty to hold society accountable for the principles espoused by the tenets of the Christian faith and their leader Jesus Christ. I believe in the universal ideas of the constitution and Christianity even if society doesn't.

You see, brother, we are the Josephs the monotheistic religions speak about. We are not just a bunch of isolated criminals; we are human beings. Yes, we committed a crime but how long must we be held responsible for it? Likewise, if Jesus Christ was physically present today, whose side do you think He would be on – ours or a bunch of hypocritical legislators who have abandoned the notion of atonement? As far as your ideas about no longer being respected, since I abandoned my devious street ways, I must enthusiastically suggest to you I'm a better individual as a result thereof. Let me tell you this, when I was a Devious Thug, my only cause for socialization with other humans was only as far as my block, community and existential (made him look up the word existential) reality afforded me.

But now that I've broadened my intellectual and moral aptitude I am considered a colleague and friend by university professors throughout America and as far as the country Denmark. Do you know where Denmark is?

CT: No, I don't, but I do know it's overseas, right?

Q: You're exactly right. When you open your mind to exploring grander ideas and concepts about life and living, you will find many loving individuals ready and willing to aid your discovery without holding your past over your head. While we are about college and university professors I would be remiss (had him look up remiss) in my duty not to give thanks and honor to the individual professors and tutors who had a personal hand in my development.

Professor Okafor (Roosevelt University); Brett Bloom (Juake Kunstakademie – Denmark); Ms. Susan Franklin, the most powerful, loving and self-assured little woman I've ever had the privilege to meet (Danville Area Community College); Mary Nichols (Danville Correctional Center Angel); Charles Davis (Danville Area Community College); Rebecca Ginsberg, William (Bill) Sullivan, Dede Ruggles, Audrey Petty, Rob Scott, Mark Micale, Rachel Rasmussen, John Lang, Cory Holding, and every tutor/instructor I have ever shared space with (all from the University of Illinois-Urbana); my Big Sister and friend Professor Karen Lyke (Ohio); and last but not least the university professor who started my thirst for knowledge was Professor Jim Thomas (NIU Sociology Department). See, young brother, what do I need with a bunch of thugs connected to the street when I'm blessed to have loving and supporting people like these in my corner? I wish I could bring street catz on the intellectual journey I'm on, not stay stagnated by cultural dysfunctions adopted by the streets.

CT: Man, you're lying; you don't have all those people in your corner.

Q: I'm not lying, those are my colleagues and friends for life. So, don't give me no bullshit about people not caring to justify thuggism over intellectual excellence. From this day forward I will help you be all you can be in prison that our environment prevented us from becoming when we were free. We now have each other, you have me to lean on and I have you. I'm responsible for my mental well-being just as I challenge you to be responsible for your own. Let's fight for excellence and kill all devious behavior hindering us from being our very best. If we do this I promise you we will change the world as we know it. Thank you for the interview.

CT: No, thank you! You helped me see some things different with this interview. I promise to start working on my devious thoughts and actions, but I'm going to need you to remind me constantly about my word.

Q: Don't worry, little homie, I got your back. It's gonna take some time getting right but I promise you that if you keep striving and don't give up, you will win the battle with self.[16]

Post Interview Thoughts

An interview like this is not a common occurrence in that most prisoners are too egotistical to open themselves up for questioning as my former cellmate did here. When I first started entertaining a book of this nature my initial thought was how wonderful it would be to conduct a similar interview with every character type for each chapter. After the negative response, I received from several chapter subjects I immediately discarded that notion; prisoners are a paranoid group. Several fears I would use the information to their detriment. An interesting fact about the incarcerated is that no matter how deep we are buried by the prison system we, illogically at times, believe there's a chance to win our appeal even when less than 5% are ever overturned. Trust is everything among subjugated men, therefore with the appellate process looming ahead most prisoners will never expose themselves in the name of some prisoner's observational book project. All wasn't lost though, I did manage to get an interview from The Pervert, The Radical, and The Religious Fanatic. Up next is the Muscle-head.

---

16 Unfortunately my cellmate got into a fight with another prisoner two months after this interview and was placed in segregation, then transferred to another prison. I hope he kept his word to rise above deviousness. I miss him.

Television Programs Watched by Conscientious Thugs

- MSNBC
- Cops
- Bait Car
- First 48
  Jerry Springer
- Maury Povich
- Love and Hip-Hop
- Real Housewives of Atlanta
- Real Housewives of Hollywood
- The Game
  Black Ink
- Bad Girl Club
- La La's Full Court Life
- Buckwild
- Hard Core Pawn
- Pawn Stars
- Mob Wives
- 106 and Park
- MTV
- VH1
- MSNBC News (Sometimes)
- Basketball Wives
- ESPN
- WGN News
- Wendy Williams Show
- Ms. America
- Victoria's Secret Fashion Show
- T.I. And Tiny Family Hustle
- Married to the Game
- CNN (Sometimes)

Magazines Read by Conscientious Thugs

- Jet
- Hip-Hop Weekly
- Vibe
- XXL
- National Enquirer
- Star
- Celebrity Slew
- Ride
- Maxim
- Playboy
- Hustler
- Black Tales
- Big Butt
- Smooth
- Blackmen
- Source
- Video Illustrated
- Essence Black Enterprise
- Chicago Tribune
- Chicago Sun-Times
- Car & Driver
- Rollingstone
- Time Magazine
- Trading Times
- Flex

Chapter 3: The Muscle-head

'We will be called to account for our use of life and our use of faith, our use of gifts, talents and/or skills. But most of all our use of time will bear witness to who we are as people and all of the above.' TFM

'No phraseology that some so-called criminologist and psychologist might use will ever be able to define the operant conditioning produced by our prison reality.' TFM

The Stress Producing Void

On a 6'x3' cot cellular subjects (prisoners) lie wasting away in cell blocks. The never-ending cycle of co-existing alongside immoral prison forms is a daily burden with physical, mental, and spiritual consequences; no one escapes the effects brought about by concrete and steel enclosures. Prison guards are no exception. But for the cell dweller, if he chooses to remain sedentary he then toys with the possibility of premature death. No matter one's intellectual and spiritual level, sedentariness is an enemy that will destroy the whole man. In an environment where power lies in its ability to restrict physical movement, recreation stands alone over all other activity in that it relieves tension of both mind and body. The confined human responds best when both mind and body find pleasing activities for diversion. Without it cellular subjects act out against the structure by hurting prison staff and similarly situated others. Recreation consequently functions as a mechanism for releasing stress; stress on any structure of confinement is synonymous with a nuclear bomb. No one wins when it is activated. For this reason, recreation has been judicially mandated for cell dwellers.

It is also true meditation and prayer are effective tools for warding off anxiety and stress, but it is my opinion no single activity works on motion-deprived bodies like exercise. This is coming from someone who takes special pride in his ability to use spiritual precepts to parry the various stimuli caused by inactivity.

A Chronology of Stress

To provide clarity to my assertion regarding stress on the body, the following chronology charts a day in the life of being confined to a 12'x9' cell that was originally conceived to house one prisoner, not two. Prison overcrowding further works in opposition to peace by enhancing stress levels and inhumane living conditions. In this regards future violence will no doubt occur, and is not totally the prisoners' fault. Here's a day in the life of a prisoner at Pinckneyville Correctional Center in Illinois.

Pinckneyville CC

12 am (midnight): institutional skin count

Comment: Some prisoners have school assignments while others work all day in the various prison jobs, helping to keep the prison complex afloat. Whether the prisoner works or not, all are equally awakened by the brightness of the count light. Stress!

3:00 or 4:00 am: another institutional count

Comment: The same scenario as the 12:00 am count except this time prisoners are deeper into their sleep pattern. The brightness of the count light disturbs your sleep 50% of the time, depending on how each prisoner deals with noise, sounds, and lights. In 16 years, I still have not gotten comfortable with the brightness or the various noises due to my security orientation and the anxiety of losing my life while in prison. Stress!

5:00-6:00 am: Prisoners are awakened for breakfast.

Comment: Due to the time breakfast is being served, 40% of prisoners forgo this most important meal for rest. Before entering prison, I never ate breakfast at 5:00 am. It was a new experience. Illinois citizens are made to believe we as prisoners receive 3 meals a day when in fact all type of stunts is pulled to deny us a balanced diet to save money that the public never sees. To date some prisons in IDOC no longer serve breakfast to prisoners. It is said that this move saves the state millions.

12-3:00 pm the prisoner is confined to his respective cell.

Comment: From noon to 3 pm if the prisoner does not have a work assignment he is confined to his cell. With Illinois prisons holding between 1800-3500 inmates/offenders, maybe only 25% at any given time will be afforded school or work opportunity. This means that most prisoners lie dormant in their cells unless they are of the character of inmates who use their prison space to workout mind or body or both. Maybe 10-15% of prisoners use their cell in the above manner. The muscle-head, the radical and the intellectual types are the ones that do.

3:30-4:00 pm: Institutional skin count

Comment: Shift change at 3:00 pm. From 3-3:30 prison guards are occupied with sorting and passing out mail. Most prisoners will agree mail time is both a time filled with excitement and/or anxiety depending upon whether the prison guard calls your name for mail. No matter how psychologically centered a prisoner appears to be on the surface, when the C/O doesn't call his name for mail a level of contemplative sadness sets in. Some prisoners never receive mail. I can't imagine what that feels like; I wouldn't want to be in his shoes. Stress! Stress! Stress!

4-6:00 pm: Count has cleared. It's now dinner time.

Comment: Just like all previous chow times (5 am breakfast and 11 am lunch), we sit around anywhere from 30 minutes to an hour waiting to be fed. By this time of the day we're hungry, sleepy and angry because we didn't receive any mail. By this time, we're just flat out stressed from the daily grind of surviving another day. Stress!

5-9:30 pm: Night activities – Shower and phone time

Comment: Every prisoner uses their time out of the cell differently. Most Illinois prisons allow prisoners who qualify out of their cells 2 ½ to 3 hours to attend night college classes. Understand: only a small percentage of prisoners will be afforded an opportunity toward higher learning. This is stressful. Prisoners are left watching other inmates attend college as they wait around for years to enjoy the same opportunity. Education ought to be the number two priority for Corrections, next to punishment. For unassigned prisoners between 6:30 and 8 pm they are released from cells anywhere from 45 minutes to an hour for showers, phone calls, or if they choose, to play cards and other games. After that it's back in our cages where stress sets in once more. Stress!

9-10 pm: Last body count.

Last count of the day before shift change, then the cycle starts all over again. This cycle plays out every day until the prisoner is released or leaves by burial box. Wow! I know. Imagine the stress of exchanging one box for an eternal one? I personally have anxiety filled days contemplating death in a prison box. Stress! Stress!

The description of the daily schedule has a dual purpose: to provide a view of a typical prison schedule, and to show the effect of stress on cellular inhabitants, and why an active body is necessary to ward off the stress of being confined over 18 hours in a cage. Again, exercise is the greatest stress reducer of all other forms. With exercise, endorphins take immediate hold of mental and physical tensions otherwise determined to destroy a healthy body. When Muscle-heads find themselves outside the margins of normalcy that is when their physical activity reaches OCD levels – at the expense of mental and spiritual well-being. In effect, the Muscle-head devalues 2/3 of his being for vanity of 1/3. Let's observe the origin of this preoccupation with physical perfection.

The Muscle-head Dilemma

Muscle-heads aren't first time offenders. They enter prison as chronic substance abusers concerned only with their next fix. The very act of ingesting harmful chemicals into the body appears to be a contradiction of the Muscle-head notion. But what happens between the time muscle-heads are snatched off the streets to the time they are released back into society is the stuff infomercials are made of. I have tried to find a logical framework by which to define this preoccupation with physical fitness and muscles that never seem to translate into a healthy lifestyle upon release. No sooner the MH is back on the street, he's playing Russian roulette with HIV, chasing promiscuous women and shooting dope in his veins.

On Familiar Grounds

Shrouded by malnutrition and low self-esteem from abusing drugs, booze, and sex, prison appears to be a saving grace for the Muscle-head. While familiarizing himself with prison rules, code and ethics, he does his best to stay under the radar from familiar felons he left behind during his last prison stint. Unfortunately, with movement throughout the various sections of prison hiding in plain sight will prove extremely difficult. Criticism is bound to follow with social interaction; it doesn't take long for old acquaintances to notice his return while eating in the prison chow hall.

Here's a typical dialogue between a Muscle-head and a fellow prisoner.

Fellow Prisoner: FP

Muscle-head: MH

FP: Man, you back?! What you didn't like it out there?

MH: Boy, quit playing so much, who the f*%k like coming to prison?

FP: Yeah, yeah, whatever nigga, why the f*%k you back then?

MH: Them people (parole officer) on some bullshit. I dropped dirty for weed and they violated me and shit. It's ah-ight (all right) tho uh nigga ain't' got but 18 months to do of this shit and I'm back up out this bitch.[17]

---

17 Observe how easily '18 months' flows off the MH's lips. When you are a perpetual criminal doing time becomes easier due to habituation but in this case, the MH's expression is merely intended to deflect shame and embarrassment for having come back to prison. Men who find

FP: Get the f*%k out of here, weed my ass! You left prison a year ago looking like Mr. Universe and you return looking like Crack head Willie. Come on man, keep it real, I ain't Allah. You know you been f*%king with that Boy and that Girl (Heroin and Cocaine). Quit bullshittin' yourself because you ain't pulling nothing over any of us doin' this shit (time).

MH: You right. I 'fell off my square' (a statement deriving from Islamic groups used by gang and prison culture describing one's ability to stand firm on principles and truth) smoking, drinking, and f*%king them bitches. I left prison thinking shit was gonna be easy for me this time then reality hit me in the head like a Louisville Slugger. Before I knew it, I was back putting heroin up my nose and sucking on that glass dick (Crack pipe). But you know me dog, I'm the shit on that weight-pile, before you know it I'll be out-lifting all your niggas in the gym in 6 months. My weight uh be back up in an uh minute – You'll see.

FP: Man, f*%k you! That's all your dumb ass think about is some weights, you need to be putting time in building yo mind up not your body. If yo dumb ass was lifting weights in the streets you wouldn't be back in prison eating this nasty ass food out the chow-hall.

MH: Kiss my ass boy, you just a hater.

FP: Wash yo ass first, nigga. Be easy my dude, I'll holla at you in the yard. Send me a kite – let me know what you need. I got you.

MH: Thanks, Bruh, you know I'm hurting.

---

themselves back in this position cringe at the thought of returning to the same correctional facility they paroled out of as criticism will inevitably follow. Fellow prisoners are brutally honest with one another. What society doesn't know is prisoners are hard on one another in this regards. Especially for prisoners serving long prison bits of twenty years or more, recidivism is unforgivable. The good thing about men who recidivate is they are examples to long term prisoners of what not to do once released.

FP: Don't trip, I got your dumb ass even tho you didn't send me shit when you went home.

MH: I know, I know, Bruh, I'm sorry.

Habitat and Habits

The above is a typical conversation played out between fellow prisoners. As is apparent, the MH's return is met with resistance even then his deflection of shame and embarrassment doesn't allow him to see the gravity of his return. In a few months, he will be back into his weight lifting routine. Weight lifting for the MH is really a form of mental disorder with OCD traits, opposed to a means of vain muscle acquisition. The points that follow further clarify the Muscle-head and his habits.

- Enduring the inevitable weeks of criticism by fellow prisoners for failing to remain free, the Muscle-head finds normalcy in his surroundings through muscle memory.

- Because a MH takes superficial pride in his physical appearance (that is, when no drugs are available) he plots to acquire items (e.g. toothpaste, face creams, deodorant, sweatpants, gym shoes, etc.) necessary to repair his appearance and thereby his image. As a repeat offender, the MH has burned bridges with his family and associates so financial support from loved ones isn't forthcoming.

- The Muscle-head uses history and charisma to acquire material 'needs' and some 'wants' from other prisoners.

- He applies for the leisure time service (LTS) position in the gym or on the yard to have greater access to weights.

- The MH knows that without food or extra sustenance, achieving a body like his past prison body will be next to impossible. He makes out a plan for caloric intake which means bumming a meal or two off other prisoners. He attends all three chow lines. He drinks all available milk at breakfast which amounts to approximately 6 8 oz.

cups or cartons. During chow time, he's further found panhandling scraps and uneaten portions off prisoner's trays which can be annoying at times. There is never a meal he doesn't find pleasing.

- He tracks down any and every fitness magazine he can locate until he's able to purchase fitness mags of his own.

- His conversation in the cell house and the gym is about weight lifting.

- Everyone he works out with or nearby he critiques them on the proper lifting techniques even if they never asked for assistance. Most often unsolicited advice leads to arguments and jarring with fellow prisoners. No one likes working out with him except prisoners similar in kind.

- When the MH is not working out via the gym, yard, cell or day room, his time is spent channel surfing programs displaying physical form, especially women's curves. Morning and late-night fitness infomercials are his favorite.

- Of all DTs, the Muscle-heads are the most comfortable in their skin. A Muscle-head has no problem complimenting another prisoner on his well-defined physique, who will then use it as motivation to correct his muscle flaws.

- Now back on top of his physical appearance, the MH walks the prison ground with an air of superiority as if everyone forgot he was a physical mess when he first arrived.

These points are played out repeatedly until the MH changes his behavior, which ultimately means overcoming his substance dependency issues.

On the surface, everything appears normal but mental instability is easy recognizable. He wears his physique like a mask and uses the PIC (Prison Industrial Complex) as a stage to further deceive himself and others – or so he thinks. Muscle-heads aren't irredeemable. In fact, they are rather charming individuals. Their character defects can be attributed to unchecked substance use, which could also mean an addictive personality type and other co-morbid issues. If IDOC and similar structures were to implement moral and/or behavioral goals before releasing such men back into society, everyone would benefit greatly. Developing a true structure for behavior modification is both morally and physically sound. Unfortunately, correctional reform continues to be unpopular legislation. It won't be much longer before the business of corrections breaks America. Maybe it has already started? Who knows? I can only see as far as my prison confines allow me to.

Television Programs Watched by the Muscle-Head

- MSNBC Lockdown
- Jerry Springer
- Maury Povich
- Love and Hip-Hop
- Real Housewives of Atlanta
- Real Housewives of Hollywood
- The Game
- Black Ink
- Bad Girl Club
- La La's Full Court Life
- Buckwild
- Mob Wives
- MTV
- VH1
- Basketball Wives
- ESPN
- WGN News
- Wendy Williams Show
- Ms. America
- Mr. Universe
- Victoria's Secret Fashion Show
- T.I. And Tiny Family Hustle
- Married to the Game
- CNN (Sometimes)
- MSNBC News (Sometimes)
- Big Ten Network
- Strong Man Programs
- Women's Volleyball
- Women's Golf
- Track and Field
- MMA/UFC/Boxing
- Fox Sports
- E!
- ENews!

Magazines Read by Muscle-heads

- Jet
- Hip-Hop Weekly
- Vibe
- XXL
- Celebrity Slew
- Ride
- Playboy
- Hustler

- Black Tales
- Big Butt
- Smooth
- Blackmen
- Source
- Video Illustrated
- Essence
- Rollingstone

- Flex
- Black Enterprise
- Body and Soul
- Men's Health

Chapter 4: The Prison Player (PP)

'Men are anxious to improve their circumstances but are unwilling to improve themselves, therefore remain bound.' James Allen

Man is not only what he chooses to be but also the things he allows himself to engage in. TFM

In His Full Glory

The Prison Player (PP) is a character whose actions and overall moral ideation I find rather despicable. It is my desire to not spend any more time than necessary with this individual since he thrives off attention and relishes being talked about no matter the manner.

The PP believes he is 'God's gift' to every woman he encounters. He uses charm, wit, and the gift of gab to disarm women to serve his superficial scheme. His gullible targets aren't just women; fellow prisoners also fall victim to the PP's charm and verbal agility as well. Any display of weakness opens the door to be engulfed by his presence. Before you know it, you're feeding him commissary and introducing him to your precious sister. This is the worst mistake any prisoner could make especially since PPs love only themselves. But if one can remain vigilant the PP character is soon discovered for the creep he is. No one can hide such foulness of character forever.

One out of ten

There she sits, alone, frustrated and impatient by her limited prospect of available men. As a little girl, she watched her mother flip-flop and cater to men like they were kings, an example she carried into adulthood that often leads to the same bad choices and abuse as her mother. Having no success with the men coming and going in her life, she decides to follow the path of a dear friend who was blessed to find her husband in prison, but what she will soon learn is finding a good husband in prison is the same as finding a needle in a haystack.

The only prisoner type I find remotely worthy to date my sister, aunt, or even mother is a rare occurrence. If you were to observe one hundred incarcerated men over the course of 1 – 3 years, maybe only one or two individuals would prove worthy enough to date a family member of mine. Therefore, it seems that 1 to 3 years is a reasonable time for observing any prisoner's behavior due to what I call 'Prison Habituation'. Prison Habituation reflects a propensity to conform to or emulate the immoral forms which permeate an unethical structure. I further submit that in a structure holding every deviant known to man, no prisoner will be able to hide behind fake morality for 3 years if he isn't truly the moral being he purports to be. For exposing the PP character, I will probably be the most hated person in prison because it potentially limits their ability to ensnare gullible, lonely, self-esteem void women for their service. I don't apologize for any exposure.

He Carves Her Up Like a Turkey

There are many ways PPs gain access to single or married lonely women (SLWs) who are open to developing a pen-pal relationship with prisoners. These ways include: the backs of magazines, pen pal newsletters, Facebook or Twitter sites, and the tried and true word of mouth, fellow prisoner homie hook-up.

With the advent of the internet the modern prisoner is more accessible than ever before. Her search for the consummate soul mate leads her to uncharted water where she represents bleeding red meat for scheming prison sharks. As she sizes up the various faces on the prison websites a handsome mug shot grabs her attention, drawing her closer and closer to the screen as if hypnotized by an invisible power. She reviews his charges, prison address and release date, then proceeds to jot down the available information for future correspondence. It takes three weeks for her to develop the courage to finally reach out to her on-the-screen aberration. Four days later the PP receives the SLW's letter during mail call and is instantly moved with excitement by the female name appearing on the envelope. He spends the next 30 minutes reading her letter repeatedly while ruminating on how to best carve up his new SLW turkey. The PP's rumination reads like this:

'Yeah – I done come up again! Who is this broad? This bitch looks like she got her shit together from what she say'n in her kite (letter) and shit. I wonder how much I can take this hoe (sic) fo (for) befo' she break (no longer communicate) out on a nigga.'

'Look at this bitch try'na act like she just happen to stumble upon a pimp accidentally while searching the website? Who this bitch think she foolin'. This broad lonely and she don' seen uh nigga picture and know uh nigga fine as hell (narcissistic) that's why she stretched out her hand to uh playa. Let me put together a scribe (a letter, a response) that will blow her f*%king wig back, uh bitch ain't gonna know what hit her – she bait on the hook. (End of rumination)

Those on the outside looking in are probably thinking there's no way men in prison talk about women in that manner! My response to those people would be 'I was merely taking it easy with the dialogue for fear of being too vulgar.' The following dialogue is between PP 1 and PP 2, sharing a conversation about the SLW letter PP 1 received. Let's refer to it as 'the philosophy of PP 1 and PP 2'.

PP1: Hey my nigga, you won't believe how uh nigga don come up again in this bitch (meaning, he has been blessed for a second or maybe a third time with an opportunity to establish social interaction with a woman).

PP2: Come on my dude, you know niggas like us (so-called Prison Players) come up all the time in this piece (prison). Why wouldn't I believe you Pimp? (Pimp is a term of endearment like buddy, homie, friend, and in the case of PPs it describes their vocation in relationship to how they treat and handle SLWs.)

PP1: You know, I'm just kick'n the shit with you, read this...

PP's take a few minutes to browse through the SLW's letter.

PP2: Player you come up for real – you got something good on your hand. Whatcha gon' do with this piece? PP1: Man, I still haven't decided how to play this angle yet. She's clearly someone I can check a bag from (a stick-up term like 'put the money in the bag' during a robbery, but now used as general slang about financial gain).

PP2: I feel you player so whatcha gon' do about the other broad on your hook?

PP1: Nigga, what the f*%k you mean: You know how we do (how PP types scheme on SLW) my dude. I'ma keep both these hoes. I'm just gonna must keep them both off balance (separated, not coming in touch with one another). Once I figure out what level this new thang is on then I'll plan my visits around their habits (habits meaning their movements, work schedules, and/or off days).

PP2: Ah-ight (all right) dawg it seem like you got you thang in order, just remember to check that bag (to get that money) and don't let these bitches check you.

PP1: Come on player, you know I do this. (He's a professional at playing gullible SLWs.) I ain't no bitch. (He isn't soft or weak on women.)

Readers on the outside looking in would be surprised to see how often the above scenario plays out daily. PPs reading this would call me a player hater for exposing their emotional, psychological, and financial abuse of women but what they can't say is I'm lying. Truthfully speaking, I took it easy on this character by not exposing how he practices similar tactics on female family members. I have witnessed PPs seduce their own mothers for financial gain. Now you see why at the beginning of this chapter I referred to PPs as 'despicable' individuals, unworthy of my observational ink, but as a principle player operating in houses of deviance I would be remiss in my duty not to showcase his vocation.

The proceeding points wrap up the PP for better or worse. Worse, in that the jig is up. It is my hope this piece has destroyed the PPs ability to use SLWs. Better in that SLWs who encounter PICs will be more informed and vigilant in avoiding clowns such as these and hopefully give the more reformed brothers in prison an opportunity for true love.

Here are the final points;

- The PP has lived a life of deception and uses charm, appearance and false moral fronts to ensnare lonely females, and sometimes male victims.

- Most PPs use backs of magazines and pen pal type websites to heighten social profile to gain access to SLWs.

- The PP is an advanced DT who uses interacting with females as a tool for escaping the reality of serving time.

- He sells SLW's dreams and makes outlandish promises without any proof or back-up for these claims.

- The PP prides himself on looks and physical features; in cases where PPs aren't physically attractive (though PPs never think they're unattractive) they use the gift of gab to overwhelm SLW victims.

- PPs are excessively self-centered and selfish and only pretend to be concerned about others.

- He has mastered the art of stagecraft; prison functions as his 'DreamWorks' studio.

- He uses words and prison politics to gain advantages which in many instances make PPs perfect tools to be used as prison snitches (Chapter 13).

- My belief is PPs suffer from minor to major multi-personality disorders: dependent, schizotypal, antisocial, histrionic, bipolar, narcissistic, and obsessive-compulsive disorder with physical upkeep and looks.

In conclusion, I hope to expose these despicable characteristics does not elicit hatred from 'sisters' for all incarcerated men. Believe it or not, some of us possess moral consciousness. Some prisoners use books, while others use weights to overcome the pressure of time; it's unfortunate that characters like PPs play with the hearts and minds of women to overcome their isolation. I apologize to all women who have ever been affected or infected by these immoral creeps. Please forgive us for their (PPs') actions. We're sorry!

.

Television Programs Watched by Prison Players

- Jerry Springer
- Maury Povich
- Love and Hip-Hop
- Real Housewives of Atlanta
- Real Housewives of Hollywood
- The Game
- Black Ink
- Bad Girl Club

- La La's Full Court Life
- La La's Full Court Life
- Mob Wives
- MTV
- VH1
- E!
- ENews!
- Basketball Wives
- ESPN
- Miami Monkey
- WGN News
- Wendy Williams Show
- Ms. America
- Victoria's Secret Fashion Show
- T.I. And Tiny Family Hustle
- Married to the Game
- Women's Volleyball

Magazines Read by Prison Players

Jet   Hip-Hop Weekly   Vibe

Tyrone F Muhammad

Men on the Inside

XXL	Source	National Enquirer (for back page into)
Celebrity Slew	Video Illustrated	
Playboy (The Bible)	Essence	Star (for back page info)
Hustler (The Quran)	Sister to Sister	
Black Tales	Hair magazines	newspapers for SLW ads
Big Butt	Black Enterprise	
Smooth	Ebony	
Blackmen	Body and Soul	

Chapter 5: The Pervert (PV)

'Nor does a pure minded man fall suddenly into crime by stress of any mere external forces; the criminal thought had long been secretly fostered in the heart, and the hour of opportunity revealed its gathered power. Circumstances do not make the man; it reveals him for himself.' – James Allen

'The weight of man's error produces a tormented soul.' – TFM

Category 5 Defined

 No prison type has caused more consternation than that of the pervert (PV); his moral disposition is an absolute embarrassment to prisoners and guards alike. The sort of crimes committed by some characters in the PV class make them highly contemptible. The fifth chapter is appropriate to cover the Perverts because there are five categories of perverts. They are: 1) The Institutionalized Freaks (ITFs), 2) The Homosexual Deviant (HD), 3) The Closet Participants (CP's), 4) The Rapists, and the most despised of PV types, 5) The Pedophiles.

Because there are so many layers in the PV classification, it was tempting to cover each of them in a separate essay. However, that would afford them more attention than necessary even though they are critical to the overall prison structure. This has been a difficult chapter to write because the perverse behaviors readily elicit moral judgments. During observing the PV types I have found myself becoming less judgmental, more understanding.

The Homo-Deviant (HD) or High-Definition (HD)

Among category 5 PVs the Homo-Deviant is the most flamboyant, his overall character personification screams 'High-Definition'. HDs are not like other homosexuals occupying prison space. Men identified as quintessential homosexual prisoners conduct and carry themselves in the most respectable and responsible manner; they understand prison code and follow it like all other prisoners. This homosexual, that is, the normal type, is conscious of how homophobic ideas play out in prison and therefore never imposes himself on other prisoners. He is respected for giving prisoners their space. For the normal type, his sole objective is to return home to his loved one(s), and not use prison acquired dysfunction for quenching his sexual appetite, although there are instances where normal types find themselves attracted to another prisoner where affection and sexual activity may ensue. However, homosexuals of the normal type are not my concern; that's a discourse for another book.

The HD type is a social pariah. He consistently violates prison cultural lines with his feminine flamboyance. Unlike the normal type, the HD sees prison as a type of buffet equipped with all the men he can eat. Heterosexual prisoners are openly proficient at avoiding this flaming individual, and I mean flaming both literally and figuratively. Everything he touches and anyone he interacts with he causes a fire of some sort. His mind is so perverted that a casual conversation with this kind unintentionally signals an invitation for a sexual tryst. Likewise, merely treating this individual in a socially respectable manner could affect the way other prisoners see and treat you, that is, if those things are important, and to most prisoners, respect is the single most important thing.

To provide a more detailed view of the HD, the following points highlight his physical features and what he goes through to achieve his look. Here they are in order of importance:

The HD goes to great effort to highlight his physical features and his appearance. The most significant material possession for any HD is his clothing. He wears the tightest pants and shirts available; if they aren't issued to him by the clothing room 2 or 3 sizes smaller then he buys them from prisoners smaller than himself.

A few prisons sell hair relaxer kits on commissary. Once or twice a year HDs buy relaxer kits where they are applied by the prisoner barber or prison cosmetology students. Each morning the HD fixes his hair in the various feminine styles showcasing bangs and baby hair slicked down on his temples with styling gel, or honey when styling gel isn't available. He plucks and arches his eyebrows twice a month then emboldens them with a black marker. He uses the black marker for an eyeliner as well.

The HD takes exceptional care and pride in his most important physical accoutrement – his lips. Whenever the opportunity presents itself, he colors them with red Kool-Aid, Jell-O, dye, red ink and on rare occasion's female officers bring in lipstick for their HD friend or possible 'snitch'. When no colorful lip accentuations are accessible there's always the tried and true, readily available Vaseline or Petroleum Jelly lip-gloss.

A Question of Morality: The HD Interview

Emerging from his cell as though arriving from a beauty salon, the HD is in full feminine mode. Directly out of his cocoon of lust stalking, prowling about for young (and some old) gullible, weak, bi-curious deviants to drain of whatever manhood they have remaining. Most HDs are intelligent Master Criminals themselves; they study subjective prey for their own pleasure just as I have studied prison subjects for my writing pleasure.

I recall 8 years ago during day room time, deep in my normal social observational mode. I guess I was staring at this HD a little too intensely, when the HD study subject, feeling the sting of my stare, turned and made eye contact with me. Not wanting him to think I was soliciting sexual favor, I quickly returned my gaze back to my research papers I had in front of me. Four or five minutes passed before the HD made his way over to my table.

I must say I was rather embarrassed by his presence. I found it difficult to be in the company of a man with feminine looks and feminine characteristics. I was seen by other prisoners as a standard for high morality, so I was afraid of tainting my character for simply being socially civil to the HD type. This dilemma is not one only prisoners encounter; society in general grapples with matters of associating publicly with those who sexual orientation or transgender is different than our own. My immaturity at the time with LGBT issues made me insensitive and judgmental.

The more I observe HD prisoners I'm convinced more than ever before that they aren't the problem in and of themselves, especially when they are just being who they are. The problem appears to be with those individuals sharing the same space with HD types and unsure of their own sexual orientation. Some of those who pass judgment on these characters are the ones in denial; they wear social masks of fear and prejudice posing as moral strength, as was my case. I feared the potential of criticism, untrue rumors and gossip from fellow prisoners who themselves were hiding behind their rough exteriors. My interaction with the HD was a learning experience that has made me more liberal in matters of politics, religion and other free human rights to choose whatever sexual orientation their hearts find desirable. Therefore, my moral conservatism ought not be a determination for how I treat and/or interact with other human forms.

After making it over to my table the HD introduced himself:

HD: Hi my name is Shay-Shay. Do you mind if I sit here with you for a minute?

Q: Why would I mind; it's not my table. I'm a prisoner like you. I don't own nothing here, not even myself.

HD: Well I had to ask because most convicts avoid sitting anywhere near me and to avoid confrontation I have learned to ask permission before standing or sitting near any prisoners who find my presence disturbing.

Q: I understand, that's prison for you. I'm fine with my manhood tho, please have a seat. By the way my name is Tyrone but you can call me Brother Malik like my comrades.

HD: Malik, everyone on the prison grounds know who you are – you stand out like hard time.

Q: I hope you mean that as an induction of my character and not a deduction?

HD: Maybe that's a bad use of phrase, what I was tryin'a say is in a small environment full of crooks, thieves and liars, righteous brother's standout. I came over here to see why you was looking at me the way you were since most guys who look at me like that only want one thing. And when I caught you staring at me I was like 'Hell naw', I know Malik ain't in to this type of shit?', so I figured why not go ask him why he's eyeballing me. Plus, I always wanted to have a conversation with you and your staring at me gave me an excuse to introduce myself.

Q: I don't wanna know why you wanted to have a conversation with me then, but that's neither here nor there now. If you don't mind can I call you by your name Shawn and not your nickname Shay-Shay?

HD: It don't matter what you call me I'm not caught up in no name. What's the matter you don't like Shay-Shay?

Q: It's not a matter of like or dislike but rather comfort or discomfort. I had a girlfriend who name was Shay who was sometimes referred to as Shay-Shay. So, calling a man by the name of my former girlfriend is quite uncomfortable. I'm not trying to be disrespectful to you and I hope you don't take it personal.

HD: I understand; no disrespect taken. This not new to me Malik, we as LGBT people have been dealing with that type of shit forever. But if it makes you uncomfortable calling me 'Shay-Shay', Shawn is fine with me.

Q: OK, then thank you, Shawn. You are right in your assessment; I wasn't staring at you because I wanted a sexual favor or anything like that nor am I passing judgment on consenting adults who engage in sexual activities. I'm writing a book about the various character types operating within what I refer to as the total institution of prison. In this regards you fit perfectly into a stratum I have termed Homo-Deviant or High Definition.[18] Do you disagree with my terminology for your type and do you mind if I use our conversation in my book?

HD: first, I believe your description of my kind or as you call 'my type' is on point. To be honest, I believe you could have been more graphic about people like me, but I see you're tryin'a be conservative. That's cool too. And no, I don't mind you using our conversation in your book so long as you don't put my full name in your project. You know how those dudes (men he

---

18 I provided Shawn an expanded explanation of the HD character and social relevance.

sneaks around having sex with) are – you'll get me killed in here cause dudes will be thinking I told on them.

Q: I'll never do you like that, you have my word. Now in observing your type and those homosexuals I describe as the 'normal type' (I explained what I meant by normal type), it appears your kind is hyper-sexual and often into confrontation over your sexual orientation and activity. Why are you so aggressive and flamboyant in this regard?

HD: See Malik, when I was younger I was a very feminine little boy. I regretted going to school because every day boys in my classroom ridiculed and bullied me. No one helped me; no one taught me how to deal with the ridicule. My teacher even thought what the boys were doing to me was funny. Every day I thought about the least painful way to commit suicide. To make a long story short after growing up and finding comfort in my sexual orientation I became vindictive toward heterosexual men, especially those machismo gay-bashing types. In my mind, I came to rationalize that men who gay bash was hiding behind their own homosexual tendencies and hated themselves for not having the courage to be who they are, therefore every chance I got to have sex with those *so-called'* (emphasis mine) heterosexual gay-baser I did. So, when you see me all flamboyant and out front with my femininity it's really an affront to those heterosexual bullies who mistreated me for being effeminate. Now that we are no longer in grammar school and are grown men these same childhood bullies sneak off in their little corners of the Joint (Prison) where they think no one is watching to f*%k me in my ass and mouth.

Q: Wow! That's graphic! Thanks for being so open and honest I would not have imagined your flamboyant way was an affront for gay-bashing bullies. Observation alone would not have revealed what you have made me aware of without an interview like this. Now earlier off the record I spoke to you about your sexual exploits and dealing with the PV character I refer to as The Closet Participant (CP). I would now like to make that conversation part of this interview without putting anyone on the spot. Because I'll never be able to get an interview like this from the CP type, can you share with me your experience and/or insight into why these individuals participate in secret and rather dangerous sexual activity?

HD: Well it's like you mentioned, these dudes come to me hyper freaky and with extreme perversity. Their only goal is to 'skeet' (ejaculate) by any means necessary even if it means sneaking around with fagots like me to do so. The only explanation I have for why dudes like these sneak around having sex with men like me is they are weak, freaky and bi-sexual, or gay individuals.

Q: OK, then so what I'm hearing you say is these men who I refer to as Closet Participants are really on the 'Down Low', so these men return to society having sex with women without informing them of their sexual exploits while in prison?

HD: Yes, they are down low guys, these so-called Macho Thugs. It's hilarious to see because they regularly pleasure themselves with my booty hole and mouth and then walk around prison as if they're not gay or bi-sexual. When I tell them they are indeed gay or bi-sexual can you believe a few have gotten angry and tried to fight me? A third of the guys I even tongue kissed after sucking on their penis.

Q: Man, Shawn, that's too much information; you don't have to be so transparent.

HD: Look Malik, how the f*%k you think you can conduct a sociological study about shit like this and not have transparency like mine?

Q: I just didn't expect you to be so raw in that way but you're right, gathering information (no matter how vulgar) is the purpose for my character observation. Please continue, I apologize for being so repulsed.

HD: It's cool. Like I was saying these men you call Closet Participants do not think they are gay or bi. In their mind, it's not sex – it's just a way to release stress.

Q: But Shawn, I don't understand that kind of logic when there are a number of other ways to release stress in prison by working out, reading, praying, or watching television; why then choose such dangerous forms?

HD: See Malik you and the people on the outside looking in are viewing this down low thing from a moral perspective. First, let me remind you that most incarcerated men aren't moral and conscientious like yourself. Therefore, the question of morality is never associated with having sexual intercourse with another man, only pleasure. You know as I do prison life is hard and activity limited, and when the opportunity exists, some prisoners use sex to escape.

Q: Well said. Tell me then, what about HIV, AIDS, hepatitis and the likes? There's no condoms in prison, does that scare you or the men having sex with you?

HD: Not really, it is what it is, we took risk with our lives by committing the crimes that landed us in prison so having unprotected sex is no different.

Q: You make a great point about risking our lives committing crime but what I'm not buying is the logical sequence of Death by AIDS vs. Death by crime, since one doesn't necessarily result in death whereby AIDS ultimately does.

HD: Put in that way I see your point so let me rephrase it in this way; I live for pleasuring myself – I'm a freak! And the men I perform sexual favors for live for pleasuring themselves, therefore pleasure comes before life. Pleasure is our life and what we live for. We just happen to be locked up. The same thing goes on in the world we just happen to be locked up right now. I'm just keeping it real with you. That's what all this observational stuff is all about ain't it? You wanted my truth, didn't you? So why you looking at me as if you're repulsed by my realness?

Q: It's not that I'm repulsed, I just never heard anyone until now express living to die for pleasure the way you just did. I imagine

71

the down low brothers or CPs are too cowardice to express their pursuit of pleasure the way you have. Furthermore, what grossed me out more than anything was the fact these perverted men sneak around having sex with HDs such as yourself then upon release from prison they have sexual relations with straight women without informing them of their sexual activity while in prison and/or their active participation in spreading HIV and AIDS. In my opinion, these men should be issued the death penalty for injecting deadly fluids into the bodies of decent women without making them aware of past sexual conduct.

HD: Man, you went off right there, you got kinda emotional huh?

Q: I know, I'm sorry. I don't have anything against homosexuals like yourself because you are true to who you are. My problem is with this Down low - Lowdown CP type who's really a bisexual posturing as a heterosexual. He's a liar who deceives his female counterpart.

HD: I feel you. The CPs I've had sex with I have told them to come out the closet and be who they are. For saying that tho I was assaulted on two separate occasions. I was even threatened with death if I said something like that ever again. Therefore, I know personally men like CPs won't ever confess to their female lovers that they were involved in sexual acts with men while in prison.

Q: I really appreciate your honesty. I'm curious about one thing tho, have you ever known CP types to knowingly have sex with someone who was HIV positive or having full blown AIDS?[19]

HD: I thought you would ask a question like this early on, I hear the rumors about me. Look Malik, what I'm about to say you must promise me again that you will not put my name in your book or say anything to the dudes you see kick'n it with me because you will get me killed. Now if you want this information

---

19 There was a rumor about this particular HD having HIV so my question in this instance was to get him to speak about his own alleged HIV infection. To my amazement he opened up about his disease.

you must make a promise to your Muslim God that what I tell you won't come back and bite me on my ass.

Q: You have my Oath to Allah and it's my ethical obligation as a writer and a novice sociologist not to link anything you say back to you, you have my word.

HD: After I tell you this I hope you don't treat me any different than you have today. Malik, I have been HIV positive since 2003 that's why I'm always in med line picking up my HIV cocktails. Now you know the rumors are true.

Q: Thank you for trusting me with your medical condition and in no way, do you have to worry about me treating you differently because you have HIV or because you're gay. That would be out of character for me but above all else you're still a human being. I'm perplexed tho by what you said which leads to my final question on this subject. The CPs you have been sexually active with – do you inform them about your HIV status?

HD: Believe it or not I do. What's surprising, even to me, is these men still have unprotected anal or oral sex with me. Why are you looking so shocked?

Q: Are you serious? These dudes are the scum of the earth! You mean to tell me even after you inform them of your HIV status they still had and have unprotected sex with you?

HD: I'm not lying to you Malik. Haven't I been one-hundred 100% truthful throughout this whole interview?

Q: Yes, you have – my disbelief arises from the fact these CP types knowingly commit suicide for pleasure. But what's hardest for me to accept is they not only endanger themselves but also the decent women they return home to. I guess it is what it is; maybe this interview will give women heads up not to have sexual relations with men coming out of prison or any man for that matter without knowing his HIV status. I must watch my back even more after this book comes out, CP types gonna kill me for exposing their down low activity like this. I guess I've done my job by exposing these individuals, now it's on the women themselves to know the sexual orientation or HIV status of the men they date, especially ex-cons. Thanks for your time, I appreciate your candor.

The Closet Participant

The above interview put forth a number of questions for debating the reasonableness of prison reform:

1) The question of conjugal visits as a means for reducing the possibility of men having sex with men and the spread of HIV.

2) The logic and ethics for providing condoms in prisons for men who have sex with men.

3) Harsher penalties for men who knowingly infect women with HIV.

4) To require HIV testing as a basis for parole for all prisoners being released back in society.

5) To create an HIV/AIDS database for prisoners who contract HIV/AIDS while in prison to be used by law enforcement or clinicians in cases where ex-cons' behavior has caused a public health concern.

6) To provide ethical and behavioral modification counseling for prisoners and/or parolees who are found with HIV/AIDS.

These issues can no longer be ignored by the public and the legislators they elect to protect them from deviant CP types. My observation suggests that CP types must be regulated due to their unchecked immorality and self-control; they are not only harmful to themselves but also the women who they become intimate with.

There isn't much more I can say about CP types that my interview with the HD hasn't already revealed, although I will add this caveat: The CP is unrecognizable. His sexual exploits are done 'on the down low', and therefore his whole character is a facade. He wears a mask to preserve his masculine mystique while performing bi-sexual closet maneuvers. In the end CPs are elusive and without form. He hides in plain sight from the public. They (CPs) are only exposed because of their confinement.

Institutionalized Freaks IF's

Up next in the PV Constellation of prison perverts are the institutionalized Freaks (IFs). The term institutionalized ought not be taken lightly as it forms the basis for the behaviors that follow. I have found the core character defect of all Deviant Thugs to be a lack of moral fortitude and/or social discipline. To submit or not to submit to moral precepts is what separates the intellectual prisoners from DTs, ALDs and MCs. The IF operates from the lowest realm of them all; they are impulsive sexual perverts who tend not to engage in bi-sexual activities like the CP kind. They are nevertheless excessively freaky individuals with no control over sexual impulse. The IF's behavior pushes and pulls on my patience like no other type. Due to close living, working and educational proximity, IFs are unavoidable. As the predominant prison type their vile vocalizations invade every social space like a locomotive; they are an embarrassment to anyone with a sense of morality. To grasp a greater understanding of this perverted foulness, the following points offer a glimpse into the IF's mindset and overall sexual pretentiousness:

- Every movie, sit-com, or television sport program, (track and field) offers an opportunity to fill the IF's lustful eyes. He especially loves to look upon the bodies of female gymnasts no matter the age. I have even heard grown men openly vocalize about having sexual intercourse with the 15-year-old gymnast Gabby Douglas. I shouldn't have to say hearing such verbal foulness boiled my blood. Women like Venus and Serena Williams have the ultimate stalking bodies. Every bodily movement, every panty peek from an elevated skirt elicit grunts and moans, like an animal in heat. The type of things IF's speaks about doing to Serena's 'Big Ass' is morally reprehensible. I recall this particular IF so engrossed in the 'Bounce Quotient' (Michael Eric Dyson) of Serena Williams buttock that out of nowhere he publicly utters these words: 'Man, look at the ass on that bitch! All I want her to do is let me eat between her ass, sweat and all'.

I don't think anyone would fault me for being grossed out by his statement, my so-called self-righteousness compelled me to ask, 'what is it about seeing a woman's ass cheeks compels you to be so verbally vile in your expression?'. Avoiding my question, the IF chimed:

'Nigga please! Stop acting so f*%king holy you know you'll eat her ass out too; you in jail ain't you? What you uh fag, you don't like women or something?'

Of course, I had to offer up a response to such ignorance. I said, 'tell me what does liking women have to do with your savage expressing of sucking on a woman's asshole? The way you're carrying on my question to you should be, do you like women, the way you treat them? You act as tho you never seen a big rear end before.'

In the end, my reproach was met with rancid sarcasm and logic fell on deaf ears. I guess it's true what the Bible says about not rebuking fools or they will hate you because they despise knowledge.

- IF's perform a number of perverted maneuvers on female officers working in the prison.

    i) They pull out their penis to urinate and/or masturbate just around the time she does her security rounds and body count.

    ii) IFs masturbate in the shower and cells while watching the coming and goings of female CO's.

    iii) IFs strategically position themselves to stalk her every bodily movement.

    iv) The same can also be said for female nurses or physician assistants. IF create pretend health issues for their penis to have it examined.

Any female encountering the simultaneous movement of one-hundred or more IF's en route to the dining hall, gym yard, or educational building is like being watched by the preying eyes of 100 hungry hyenas. I imagine this to be rather intimidating for passing female staff and guest. The simultaneous twisting and turning of one hundred heads eyeballing female crotch, chest and buttock is chilling, reprehensible and embarrassing. This single act more than any other has a definitive way of reminding you that prison is unruly, complex, and full of savages until proven otherwise.

- Female volunteers from religious leaders to teachers enter prison for the sole purpose of imparting useful information and services to disenfranchised men. Unfortunately, to teach the few sincere prisoners, they must endure every preying, ever-stalking eyes of perverted IF's.

Intellectual Frustration with IF Characters

For the intellectual prisoners who take exceptional pride in social reformation through self-development and educational programs, the actions of IF's are frustrating because prisoners are lumped into the same pot of behavioral soup. Prisoners who do everything required of them by the institution are still penalized for the actions of others. Once again productive and conscientious prisoners are just as disturbed by the actions of IF's as those females enduring the disrespect to service the few desiring changes.

I recall on two occasions having to confront IF's about their disrespectful and reprehensible behavior. The first time was when I worked as a T.A. For Career Technology Class at Danville CC instructed by two wonderful black females. As the story goes, both women were often required to leave their desk to assist class participants with various computer lessons. This IF locked his eyeballs between the legs of one instructor from the moment she stood up until the moment she sat down as if in some type of hypnotic trance.

Observing his actions, the entire duration I asked him if he would follow me into the hallway so we can talk about something without disturbing the class; he obliged. Once in the hallway we discussed what I bore witness to and his classroom ethics. He fought me on my observation for a minute or so before finally acquiescing and apologizing for his actions.

My second IF confrontation occurred while attending the Education Justice Project's (EJP) Resource Room where books, literature and other materials relevant to semester course requirement is located. In addition, the Resource Room is a comfortable place to study and receive assistance from University of Illinois provided tutors, professors and volunteers.[20] This student IF decided he would use valuable Resource Room time to exercise his inordinate lust on one of the female tutors. By prison standards she was rather attractive, a fact not lost on the IF she was tutoring. After watching him stare for approximately 30 minutes at the tutor's breast while pretending to need help with his assignment I kindly motioned him to the hallway to have a conversation. We talked for about 15-20 minutes on the value of education and not destroying our educational program by being pervertish with professors and tutors. After apologizing and promising never to do it again, the IF asked me 'how did you know I was stalking old girls tits, was I that obvious?'. 'No, you weren't; I've just made it a priority of mine to protect our educational program, so stuff like you're doing is hypersensitive and stands out. Therefore, if you don't change your behavior I will inform Ms. Ginsburg that you are not mature enough to be a part of EJP's learning environment.' The student IF understood my concern and promised to bring his lust under control and begin taking his educational opportunity seriously. Although I wasn't going to

---

20 The Education Justice Project is a University of Illinois sponsored prison Bachelors program founded by Rebecca Ginsburg and others. Rebecca Ginsburg believes true reform and/or justice is achieved through educational opportunity and not only punishment. Furthermore Ms. Ginsburg believes education is a human right and the truest way to achieve equality. EJP is the best thing that has happened to Illinois prisons and prisoners. EJP needs more support from the public.

simply take his word for it, I kept my foot on his perverted neck until he became one of EJP's best students.

It's apparent men like these have some kind of Impulse-Control disorder. Not all IF's are lucky to have someone intervene in their affairs, for the most part prisoners try not to interfere in other prisoners affairs, but in situations such as the preceding example where one prisoner's action can affect an educational program that all prisoners benefit from its wise for somebody to intervene.

Unfortunately, throughout the prison population hundreds of these individuals go unchecked and thus carry their perverted tendencies back to the public. The prison structure is more responsible for fostering these freaked out character types than the prisoner himself. Denying prisoners, the natural use of sexual energy via conjugal visits or other forms of social interaction with the opposite sex encourages perversity to satisfy some kind of sick judicial decree. Not to mention prisoners are getting younger and younger with hormones racing from 0 to 60, plus with the daily bombardment of sexual images on television and in magazines, it's no wonder sex deprived IF's act in the manner they do. In truth, I am surprised women volunteers aren't sexually assaulted more often by sex crazed IF's.

The Pedophile and the Rapist

No two groups are more despised and hated by the prison population than the Pedophile and Rapist. The only thing protecting these prison types from being executed by other prisoners is the Law.

When I first entered prison almost two decades ago, men such as these were shunned and frowned upon by all prisoners; their actions were unacceptable and despicable. Nowadays this group of prisoners are coddled and protected by the Courts and prison apparatus, even correction officers pamper these individuals. It's no wonder Pedophiles and Rapists come in and out of prison committing sex related crimes repeatedly until the

State finally puts them away for victimizing women and kids. Notwithstanding the prisoners who should be given an opportunity at freedom are left rotting from old age. This point is further exacerbated by the fact that taxpayers are left footing the health care cost of geriatric prisoners who have long aged out of criminal deviancy.

Penological logic would be better served by monitoring every prisoner's conduct not just Pedophiles and Rapist who enter and leave prison houses. The real tragedy being that with all the legislative measures in place to protect the public from sexual predators Correctional Institutions still release PVs to commit the same crime over and over until such an act causes permanent, irreversible damage to women and children.

Personal Disdain and Never-ending Story of Pain

My experience with these types is rather personal and disheartening. When I was 13 or 14 my mother was a victim of rape, even as an adult I am still affected by that incident. It is my premise my youthful brush with crime and the devious behaviors that follow directly correlate with the rape my mom endured. Until this book I have never openly expressed to her how that rapist not only destroyed her innocence but mine as well. All these years I have held myself responsible for my mother's pain. As the story goes:

It was a hot summer's night, my mother, sister and I lived in an apartment building with my grandmother across the street from Sangamon Discount Liquors on 59th Street in Englewood, (a section of Chicago). Whenever the weather permitted my uncles and cousins who lived around the corner would hang out on the front porch for most of the night.

Being the curious, nosy and mannish little boy, I was, I wanted to be in on every conversation even if it meant bearing the brunt of most jokes. When it got dark, my mother would instruct me to come in the house for bed, but on this day my uncle Shawn told her to allow me to stay up and that he would look after me and send me upstairs in an hour or so. One hour turned into two, two into three, and before I knew it was three in the morning. If it was on the weekend then time wouldn't be an issue, but it was a weekday and that meant I had to walk my mother to the bus stop and go to school.

My mother was a hardworking, strong-willed, independent single parent who worked two jobs to support my sister and me. For as long as I can remember Englewood has always been a crime ridden Ward. Every morning I would walk my mother to 59th and Halsted to catch the first bus in a series of bus and train rides to arrive at her first work destination. I took great pride in protecting my Mom in that way, even from the strangers who would become her boyfriends.

Anyway, my routine of protecting and seeing her safely off to work was disrupted by my desire to be grown for a night. When the time came to walk her to the bus stop like I have done hundreds of times, I was too exhausted from my late-night activity that I was incoherent. What I remember most was my mother saying, 'Boy, I told you to get up and walk me to the bus; it's time for me to go to work. I'm not going to keep asking you to get up. Every time I get my check can't nobody beat you begging for new gym shoes – Yo mannish ass shouldn't've been up all night being grown. Now get up, boy!' True to her word, she stopped asking me to get up and went off into the early morning hour without her protective son in tow.

Approximately two hours or so elapsed when the commotion of police walkie talkies and angry family members woke me. Wiping the sleep from my eyes and finally gathering myself I headed in the direction where the bulk of the commotion was coming from. Once in the living room I immediately noticed my mother wasn't at work and surrounded by female family members and police officer taking statements. Shocked by the police presence, I asked my uncle, 'what's going on'? He said: 'your mother was raped. A man put a butcher knife to her neck, walked her to an alley and raped her while she was waiting on the bus.' Hearing my uncle's words sent chills of guilt and rage so deep into my soul I almost fainted.

Making eye contact with me, my mother turned to her sister and said, 'don't let my son see me like this', and turned her broken body to the side. Talking about it now still produce great sadness in me. With all my mother had just been through there she was trying to shield me from the pain she was experiencing. There I stood holding and am still holding myself responsible for what that sick pervert took from my mom and me. All she asked for was that her son walk her to the bus stop and I failed her in that simple task, a failure that has haunted me for 30 years. Writing about the incident now is my first open expression of the pain and hurt I've felt. Psychologically, as it has been shown, Rapists not only destroy their rape victims but loved ones as well. I can honestly say that one incidence destroyed my innocence and ultimately set the course for a life of deviousness and violence that followed.

My anger toward men and the violence I inflicted on them as a gang banger teenager can be traced back to that experience, along with the guilt I felt for having dropped the ball protecting my mother, my Queen. I recall roaming the streets at 13 with a .22 special handgun I stole from my Uncle looking for anyone fitting the description of the rapist, even if the man I happened to stumble upon was the wrong man, my hurt and pain would have exposed that individual to unjustified harm.

After I spent more than 3 hours roaming the streets in a vindictive rage my mother sent my uncle to bring me home. Happy to see my mother back to her normal strong self (or at least she wore a mask of normalcy) I remember her hugging and kissing me as if I was the one victimized hours ago. Sensing my pain and shame she whispered in my ear, 'Tyrone, it's not your fault what happened and stop blaming yourself.' At that moment those words were the most soothing words I've ever heard, tho they were short lived. In the end as it stands today concerning issues of rape and pedophilia my emotions are stirred to anger.

In my defense I am more mature now about dealing with men incarcerated for rape and/or pedophilia, where years ago that wasn't the case, I wanted to physically hurt those prisoners I encountered who were discovered to have sexually assaulted women and kids. I know I'm not God, Judge or Jury of these individuals, but like any decent human being with a conscience and emotions, I'm rather disturbed by the physical violence perpetrated by those types. Wanting to understand why pedophiles in particular preyed upon the bodies of children I sought to interview a prisoner convicted of pedophilia and/or criminal sexual assault on a minor. This interviewee was charged and convicted in two separate incidents for molesting two young boys. I present the Pedophile Prisoner (PP) interview.

Q: Thank you for having the courage to put yourself out like this especially given how prisoners such as myself view and treat your kind. Let's get right to it. To start is this your first case like this?

PP: No it isn't.

Q: Then tell me how many times have you been convicted for sexually assaulting a child and what were their ages?

PP: I'm embarrassed by it now but in my sickness I sodomized two young boys age 6 and 9.

Q: OK now – you don't know how you just hit me in the chest with that revelation.

PP: You said you wouldn't judge me if I did this interview with you.

Q: I'm not judging you but I am a human being with emotions who happens to love children. At the time we talked about my interviewing you I wasn't aware you had two pedophile type cases. You just informing me about the second molestation case kind of shocked me. Please forgive me for being unprofessional; that won't happen again. I'll try to stay focused on the issue no matter what you reveal. Please continue being open and honest to my line of questioning. I'm sorry for interrupting you with my sociological immaturity.

PP: Don't trip (meaning, not to worry), I guess your response is normal. I understand.

Q: You mention that this is your second time in prison for molesting another child. Not to be funny or anything but tell me this why did you feel the need to sodomize a second little boy? Wasn't one enough?

PP: It was nothing like that man! When I was released from prison my thoughts wasn't on going up in some kid butt, my thoughts were on surviving and staying free. I had no intention on coming back to prison for another pedophile charge.

Q: Clearly your intentions weren't in line with your actions. What made you violate another child and who was the second child you victimized?

PP: I'm sick man. I know I'm sick. I would be the first to tell you men like me should never be released until there's absolutely no chance we will do something like this again. I will never forgive myself for what I did to my sister's little boy. I understand why she hate me because I hate myself. But Malik, I'm sick. The problem is, they knew I was sick before they released me.

Q: Back up for a second. You said they knew you was sick before they released you. What do you mean by that and who are they?

PP: They are the prison, psychiatrist and parole officials who were assigned to meet with me once a month. I told my psych about the anxiety and dreams I was having about touching on boys before I was released. I acknowledge my wrong but prison officials also bear some blame for releasing me before I was ready.

Q: So are you ready to be released now?

PP: No! I can honestly say no, I'm not.

Q: I couldn't've imagined you would say no, but at least you know yourself. Now let me take you back to a previous statement you made. You said a minute or so ago that you destroyed your nephew's life. Do you mind sharing with me what happened in the case of your nephew and how you came to victimize him of all people.

PP: It's not like that. I didn't purposely seek to molest my sister's child. I told you before, I'm a sick man.

Q: Yes, I heard that but even sick men can be discriminating with the crimes they commit. For instance, a man who has a sickness for alcohol doesn't necessarily walk around drinking gasoline because it has alcohol in it. So what inner Demon of Deviance would cause an uncle to violate his own nephew?

PP: Well I guess you can say I saw an unchallenged opportunity given my nephew trusted me. What else can I say, I'm a sick individual. Every day I punish myself for destroying my nephew's life. On top of that, I lost my entire family because I'm a perverted freak. Yeah, I'm doing time for my crime but losing my family is a lifelong prison sentence. In my mind tho I'm in a prison within a prison.

Q: That's unfortunate but at least you're now taking personal inventory of your bad behavior and subsequently recognize the need to get help for what you yourself call a sickness. It appears you're on the right course so who am I to judge, everyone in this world have their own Demons to deal with. Years ago I wouldn't be found speaking to someone such as yourself because in my mind you would be worthy of death for what you did to your nephew. Today I see things much differently where people like you are the product of a sick garden (society). However, I'm hopeful interviews like this and subsequent others will foster broader discussions around child molestation and rape issues. Thank you for being open and honest. Maybe something meaningful can be drawn from it.

Finding Closure and Release

When I first decided to interview the Pedophile in the PV category, I did so believing I could be professional and emotionally void but that was next to impossible. Initially I wanted to interview two men who were convicted of rape, but my mother's rape memories got the best of me so I decided against that, and went with the Pedophile. No chapter has stirred more emotions than this one, although working on this chapter has allowed me to grapple with the hidden guilt of not being there to protect the one person who has always protected me. I now know it's not my fault; rapists rape but that doesn't make it any less painful especially when the rape victim is your mother.

The older I become it seems that women's social, economic and biological issues are a growing concern of mine. On one hand I see women equal in life, liberty and the pursuit of happiness alongside men. But on the furthest spectrum of my moral-protectionist scale I see women as physically incapable, vulnerable and helpless against savages like these without the protection of men. Maybe this statement sounds a bit chauvinistic in tone but I assure you it comes from a pure space. If brain power were the scale by which social, political and economic viability are determined, then women would be the leaders of this world. Unfortunately brain power takes a backseat to physical attribute, military might and patriarchy. This point further bears witness to our (America's) excessive engagement with war and all things sports. Likewise, with the inordinate focus on female bodies in magazines and television, it's no wonder sick men like these are overly freaked out over body parts.

Viewed in this light and with the ever increasing assault on moral integrity, disregard for female bodies will continue as evident by the growing number of sexual predators entering prison. I have the unwanted privilege of living with these ultra-perverts every day. That given, if being viewed as a chauvinist for wanting to protect women and children from what my mother suffer through at the hands of sick-sex crazed maniacs, then I welcome the term. Observation in this instance must translate into protecting women and children. Who would argue with this?

Chapter 6: The Liar

"All of us are masters at telling lies. We are better liars than we are Christians, Jews, Muslims or neighbors." TFM

"What we perceive as truth is without doubt true, even if our perception is based on a lie." TFM

The Liar! A vociferous sack of lying contradiction on all levels of physical confinement. It is true all prisoners at some point use lying as a tool for survival, although the Liar has mastered it as an art form. He lies even when doing so further exasperates his personal peace and security. As an inherent quality of prison, lying functions as a social neutralizer for staff and prisoner alike. From the urban city streets where crimes are committed to the courthouses where criminals are prosecuted, prison in and of itself is an ever evolving lie organized around politics, law, and what I describe as unspoken policies for eliminating urban scum, aka black and brown thugs. With this view out front, lying then appears to be a necessary evil for maintaining social control and separation. Within prison this dynamic is given a number of terms. Prison Staff hides behind Intel and Ethical guidelines aka Departmental Rules (DR's), while prisoners themselves hide behind universalized codes such as not associating with prison staff, thereby giving the appearance of snitching, aka 'Telling Something'. I will expound more on snitching in Chapter 13 Institutional Slaves (IS).

Liar 4.0

Deception and lies are hallmarks of criminal activity; the greater the lie, the greater the crime tends to be. Most crimes and the individuals who commit them are economic in nature. The exceptions include murder, rape, and pedophilia, although some murders that are gang related often times stem from creating and protecting drug territory, therefore murders are more nuanced than the act itself depicts.

But the question here isn't about a particular crime but rather the activity of lying as a staple for criminals confined to prison houses. Viewed from a psychological perspective we then know Liars lie to cover their apparent frailty. Now the psychological effect on incarcerated bodies makes living in the body even more complex. In this case prisoners are forced to deal with the ramifications of their crime and who they will ultimately become or be once in prison. Some prisoners arrive at a healthy space soon after entry; unfortunately the vast majority are unable to effect behavioral change. To compensate for their character defect, liar types embellish about their crime, their financial status, and their social standing in the world they were removed from. Liars place themselves in close proximity to those prisoners who are financially competent who range from the 'Big Time' drug dealers to the most affluent Gangster, Hustler, or Pimp from Chicago. Liars use the examples of successful street thugs as proof positive that lying and scheming do pay off even if it eventually lands them in prison. For the Liar, nothing is ever personal . Every word proceeding from his mouth is for self-edification and scheming, except for when his lying has run amok and thus leads to some kind of physical confrontation.

In the abyss of confinement where prisoners strive for normalcy count on the Liar's fallacious interjections to disrupt the spirit of a dialogue. He can't help himself. His lack of self-esteem lends further credence to his verbosity. A conversation with this type is a constant screening process to assess what to accept or not accept as truth. And if you're thinking why not just avoid this individual, I would say to you, he's unavoidable. The Liar is a master of making himself the focus of every social circle, all days he talks people, places, and things. The following points provide a clear detailed view of the Liar:

- From day one of entering prison he lies about the nature of his offense even when no one inquires about the nature of his incarceration.

- He immediately upon entering prison locates his special crowd. If he is of the Snitch type he gravitates towards prison authorities in an effort to curry favor for future service.

- He lies about his skills and abilities to gain access to certain prison jobs.

- He lies about his education/learning but is often found without a GED. When confronted on this point he conjures another lie to camouflage his original lie that goes something like this: "These people (Prison Officials) bogus. Them people lost my high school records and told me I have to take my GED all over again. It ain't nothing tho the work is easy." (Note: while he's making this statement he has been in GED class two years and failed the test 2 or more times.)

- He lies about the sophistication of his criminal activity but is often found to be a Rapist, a Pedophile, and a substance abuser who performs petty thefts and home invasions to support his drug habit.

- He lies about his association with urban street thugs to establish social relevance during his prison time. Since all things criminal are local, deviants find fondness for notorious Pimps, Drug Dealers, and Murderers. No matter the community or gang affiliation, name association with notorious street thugs carries broad weight with others prisoners even if the association is false.

- He lies about his familial closeness but is rarely seen using the phone, going on visits, or even receiving mail.

- He lies about his past and present financial status but is seen panhandling fellow prisoners for food, clothing, and other commissary goods for survival. He uses new gym shoes and clothes to give the appearance of worth but what is not seen is:

- How the Liar uses the gift of gab to swindle other prisoners out of commissary items.

- How the Liar saves up his prison pay (that ranges from $10 - $45 a month) to purchase material items; it can take up to 6 months for this individual to purchase a single pair of gym shoes but once he purchases them he walk around like he just bought $3000 alligator skin shoes.

- How the Liar uses fake generosity to trap other prisoners into doing the same for him. He gives of the little he has in order to secure a lot in return. Once he's able to determine the financial usefulness of those he associates with he works his charm to perfection. He does his whole prison sentence on the backs of fellow prisoners.

- How the Liar searches out and befriends those prisoners whose sentences are nearing an end for the purpose of retrieving items (shoes, clothes, food, etc.) they may leave behind.

The above points do not cover the Liar activity in entirety but enough details are put forth to provide a pretty good feel for this character, therefore I won't spend another second wrestling with the Liar. I now present The Religious Fanatic.

Chapter 7: The Religious Fanatic (RF)

If a man live his life in submission to the laws of the universe, God, etc., then and only then will man live in peace. – TFM

It is through pure thought that I change myself and the world around me – TFM

My ultimate goal is to spiritually move beyond my ability to be physically relevant. – TFM

Your personality provides onlookers a glimpse into your soul. – TFM

To cope or not to cope – that is the question

The systematic crushing of the human will to live is never felt more than when entangled by prison bars. Once inside, the occupants of entanglement must resolve to find relevance within all domains of prison life or total death ensures. There's no middle ground. Where the spirit of death assails, prisoners have two choices, to find purity within then proceed to control its outcome, or become engulfed by the ever-gyrating pulse of prison's structural falsities. Likewise, to contend with the daily permeation of prison permanence, some prisoners find relief in entertainment and prison folly such as TV watching, games of chance, and the excessive edification with body parts via weight lifting and visual pleasure obtained from stalking women in TV and magazines. Notwithstanding, there are those prisoners who challenge structural falsities through a process of mind edification. The Religious Fanatic (RF) compensates for structural dysfunction by immersing himself in religious dogma from sun up to sun down.

In plain sight

On first encounter, the RF's character personification appears commendable, but being in his presence for any length of time soon reveals a personality more convoluted than the initial engagement suggests; a character stained by a dogma that's multiplied and extremely self-effacing; a telltale sign of complexities sheltered within monotheistic cracks and creeds. I had never before witnessed religious convolutedness on this level until I entered prison. From Christianity to Islam, the RF's mystic rapture is like a movie plot, where the actors' bodies have been invaded by aliens of the Holy Kind. Though there are various degrees to the RF's religious fixation my point here is merely to convey prisoners who have so picked up religion as a means toward self-reflection and transformation that they take religious convergence to heights unlike any I've witnessed in free society, often times to a point of radicalism. I will discuss radicalism further in chapter 8, the Radical.

Style vs. Substance

In all chapters preceding this one it has been my writing style to show the actions of each character type. I will do no less here. In doing so I have one caveat, that the reader view my treatise on the RF as an example of how religions act more as a coping mechanism on incarcerated bodies, rather than a function for spiritual elevation. In this case, the men who gather around religion use it like a psychiatrist would the prescription Haldol on a patient affected by schizophrenia. Viewed from this vantage point, religious tenets as a basis for spiritual enlightenment and/or ethical reinforcement, in my opinion, are only relevant with those prisoners I classify as intellectual in chapter 11. For the Intellectual, spiritual formulations are an intricate part of his character reformation, and thus finding one's spiritual pathway is a process most prisoners will never travel unless beckoned by the possibility of death, i.e. cancer, HIV, and other such terminal illness, only then will his eventual meeting with eternity cause him to entertain spiritual relativism.

Religious Functionalism

For most incarcerated men, alcohol, cocaine, heroin, marijuana and now the craze that is popping pills, were used as a crutch for escaping life's hardships. But understand, once in prison, life's hardships don't become less pronounced and disappear; they take on other forms, the greatest being stress caused by physical limitation which essentially destroys one's motivation to be creative in thought and actions. Furthermore a restricted body acts on the human soul like kryptonite to Superman. As a function of survival once physical movement is restricted the prisoner must find alternative mechanisms for coping or lose his mind as described in chapter 3, the Muscle-head.

75% of RFs find mental solace in the monotheistic brand Christianity, although Islam within prison structures is quickly becoming the go-to religion for incarcerated bodies. Out of all other religious fanatics those choosing Christianity as a means for escape are the most extreme in religious functionalism.

These men in every aspect are disconnected from the real world as we know it. Engaging in a simple conversation with the Christian RF is like being transported to a religious convent. Every sentence proceeding from his mouth is incomplete if it's not accompanied by the utterance of God, Jesus or the Holy Spirit. He wears Jesus on his sleeves like cuff links attached to a shirt. Everyone he shares space with painfully endures his incessant incantations. His constant biblical invasion on the ears has unintended consequence in that his fanaticism further isolates prisoners from religion, as opposed to ushering them to religious ranks. For the RF, religious loquaciousness has successfully rendered the utterance of "Jesus" on par with other despicable words like 'Ni....' and 'fa....'

I know this comparison sounds rather harsh to those unfamiliar with prison culture, but for those forced to endure the AR-15 ear assault of Jesus, the occasional N and F word is a welcome sound. To put the RF's Jesus offensive in perspective, I have included the following dialogue. I call it the Jesus Offensive.

The Jesus Offensive

Religious Fanatic: RF

Fellow Prisoner: FP

FP: What's up my brother, how's things going?

RF: Praise the Lord – all things are well for those who love the Lord Jesus Christ and submit to His will. It's not my will it's the Lord's will that I live for. I'm of the peace makers for Jesus said in Matthew 5:9, "Blessed are the peacemakers for they shall be called the Children of God", and as a Child of God I am blessed and highly favored. (Note: the RF spends part of his day learning Bible verses to use for moments like this to impress others with his biblical knowledge.)

FP: That's good. I'm happy to hear everything is well with yourself. It sounds like you are finding substance with God. (Note: the FP only makes this statement for appeasement and not necessarily due to a genuine interest in the RF's religious odyssey.)

RF: Yes Sir, Jesus for me is everything. He's the way, the truth and the light. Jesus says in Matthew 10:37 and 38 that "he that love his father or mother more than Him is not worthy of me; and he that love his son or daughter more than Him is not worthy of Him." and that we must 'take up our cross and follow after Him'. So yes, I'm taking up my cross and leaning on the Lord's instructions, not my mother or father's . This I do for the love of the Lord.

FP: I see you man, I see you knee deep into your religious thing. I'm not mad at you for that. (Note: what he's really saying in his head is, 'this Ni.... crazy for drinking that Jesus Kool-Aid the way he has', and is merely looking for an opening to transition the conversation.) Did you watch Obama's speech last night? He really did good I thought.

RF: I glanced at it for a minute or so but in truth the TV was watching me while I was reading my word. I make it my business to get between 10 to 20 chapters in before I turn in for bed. Reading my bible is more important than Obama or any other political figure. Obama is going to hell right along with those white politicians – he's no different than the scribes and Pharisees Jesus spoke about in the Bible. Politicians are a bunch liars; the only one I'm putting my trust in is my Lord and Savior Jesus Christ. (By this point the FP has become frustrated with RF's overemphasis on all things religion, as indicated by his next response.)

FP: Alright man, would you get your Jesus panties out your ass! I was just trying to have a conversation with you, homie. Why is it that every time someone has a simple social exchange with you , you feel the need to inject Jesus in everything?

RF: Jesus is my everything. Jesus is what I want to talk about. He's the way, the truth, and the light of the world, and all things in it, so why not talk about Jesus in all things?

FP: Because everybody's not in to that Jesus shit the way you are into it, so why force Jesus on everyone you talk to? Don't you think you need a little balance?

RF: Because Jesus instructs me as a believer to bear my cross and carry His word to the four corners of the earth. The word will save mankind from their sin. Jesus is the only balance I need.

(The conversation now became heated and personal as it always does when religion and politics are out front. Prisoners tend not to function well when disagreements arise and can become verbally abusive towards one another.)

FP: The 4 corners of the earth? Nigga, your ass ain't never left the 4 corners of your block. I hear you speaking all this Jesus shit but this is your second prison bid for molesting a kid – what does Jesus say about that since you always judging everyone else based on what Jesus said?

RF: That was a low blow, but "no weapon formed against the righteous shall prosper". I'm no longer that person. I've been saved by the blood of Christ and have been made a new creature when I confessed to Jesus my sins. He said to sin no more and all is forgiven.

FP: So Jesus said that to you, huh? Jesus might have forgiven you but the families of your victims haven't. Plus what type of sense are you making, talking that Jesus blood saved you shit when in the real world that stuff ain't gonna fly. And besides, how is it that Jesus blood is able to save you but it's ineffective in saving those kids you molested? That Jesus stuff might be able to fool those poor gullible religious volunteers from outside but to us game conscious prisoners you sound like an illogical clown. So cool it with all that Jesus shit when you're talking to me – I'm not buying your God games.

RF: I hear you; you're just a Christian hater. Don't nothing faze me tho, because I've been anointed and appointed by the Spirit of Christ and as long as Jesus blood runs through me then that all the forgiveness I need. Hallelujah!

The above scene is not unlike the many which play out on a daily basis. Conversations like these occur all the time. Prisoners often challenge one another in their own logical way to take responsibility for their actions. In this case this particular

RF hides behind the blood of Christ and his so called religious transformation. Due to his ever fanatic expression of all things Christ, more often than not the RF type will encounter confrontation whenever he engages in dialogue with fellow prisoners. The scenario around this individual is an ever changing lie, fueled by religious proselytism which heeds only to the voice of Christ. In this case, as in all other instances of deviant observation, the RF's place within prison culture is equally relevant especially given the hardship of serving time that is often void of outside support. Therefore loneliness and abandonment are an open enemy to all prisoners big or small, learned or unlearned, sane or insane. In this regards, Jesus is a neutralizing force but only for those individuals who have come to know Him (Jesus) from a space of spiritual practicality and not one from insanity masquerading as some divine revelation or intervention.

Chapter 8: The Radical

Black men caught in the criminal justice system are like fishes caught in the fisherman's net. TFM

Being incarcerated is not a reality, it's an illusion. Prison guards conform to an illusion of control, prisoners outnumber those placed in charge over them 10 to 1. TFM

The social anatomy or the anatomy of blackness seems to be tied to the prison industrial complex. TFM

A deprived human going in the correctional system and a depraved, vindictive human coming out; also known as the natural disaster of broken souls abandoned by a decadent democracy. TFM

Life for prisoners is like a game of craps. They can never win when those who control the game are playing with loaded dice. TFM

A Radical Journey

Travel with me if you will as we journey to a mind affected by four concrete walls, steel doors, rampant ignorance, and institutional injustice on every level of human interaction – a journey shaped by a nation founded on murder and imperialism which purports liberty and justice for all. Such a fallacy of democratic purity is propagated through the various socio-political outlets to prevent the discovery of truth.

From concrete to steel structures the Radical speaks out against the immoral actions of a fallen giant that has long been contaminated by the stench of its own bowels. In his subterranean chamber of isolation and despair the Radical's body and actions are regulated by inanimate materials obstructing his physical motion.

The ill intent of this intelligent design puts asunder anyone or thing so daring as to traverse beyond its construct. And depending on the quality of mind prison overseers can make physical isolation less cumbersome or hell in a hole. Prison is a state of second death where motionless bodies seek conformation for their subjugated state. But while drawing from his awakened consciousness, The Radical soon discovers the beauty of death. With physical bondage, The Radical grows to embrace the possibility of death in a box. The Radical knows that while time destroys the body, in his awakened consciousness he finds mental and spiritual health.

The Radical Defined

Prison bars are enough to turn the staunchest patriot into a radical. When the human body is brought under the burden of material obstruction the mind naturally seeks avenues for flight as it struggles to survive. The Radical's most important possession is social defiance, a trait influenced by environmental dysfunction. To understand the Radical we must consider the factors giving rise to this type. They are:

1. Most Radicals come from single parent households.

2. They were inquisitive young boys who came to know at a young age the social, political, and economic deficiencies of their upbringing.

3. Being more conscious than their grammar and high school peers has gotten them into trouble for having the audacity to challenge information imparted by the teacher. Thus attending school acts as a hindrance and not an intellectual obligation; therefore they drop out.

4. The Radical is critical of politics and sees it as a trap against the disenfranchised. He is extremely pessimistic of politicians' will or ability to serve the interest of black and brown citizens.

5. He sees law enforcement and enforcers as governmental vehicles for performing genocide on communities of color.

6. He believes laws are for the poor and that rich people aren't governed by the same rules and laws poor people are beholden to.

7. He believes financial autonomy and self-determination is the only cure for white patriarchal rule.

8. The lack of respect for the rule of law causes Radicals to take penitentiary chances with his freedom.

9. Serving prison time only elevates the Radical's social ideas and disapproval of America's one sided democracy or Demon-cracy (rule of the Devil) by

   a) Witnessing the unchecked power of correctional staff who systematically violate prisoners' due process in every area of prison existence without legal or political consequences

   b) A dysfunctional parole process that's biased, condescending and serves as an impediment to reform rather than a healing for incarcerated bodies.

   c) An environment promoting mental and physical ailments.

   d) The intentional dumbing-down of an entire prison population through inaccessible learning opportunities.

   e) The systematic separation of minority men from family members and communities from which they come. (This act ultimately has an adverse effect on poor communities and essentially punishes not only the prisoner but the human lives connected to those serving time. It perpetuates poverty and desperation, only leads to further social disintegration.)

   f) The never ending recidivism of men experiencing the inability to gain meaningful employment after being released.

   g) Bearing witness to over-paid babysitters. Prisoners pretty much run themselves and they are the ones who keep prison internal mechanism running.

10. Prison for the radical as well as the Intellectual acts as an incubator for developing his ideas – a Deviant University of sorts, in contrast to a structure for

punishment, and certainly not a place for remediation or reform.

President George W Bush once proclaimed that prison produced enemy combatants, a proclamation I agreed with long before it was uttered. In a 2000 essay I wrote extensively on the unchecked, un-monitored minds of prison dwellers that are abandoned and likewise left to their own devices to cultivate destructive identities without positive input from correctional structures. Point #10 provides a framework by which to gauge the Radical's evolution. For the Radical, prisons are foundations for social inclusion where prison bars have the unintended consequence of creating a Social Monster or a unique type of Mental Genius. I have found the latter to be especially true with this type but unfortunately, it is the Social Monster that stands out for prison officials and Government Agencies (i.e. FBI, CIA, ATF).

And Then There Were Three

Hailing from communities where politics fail in its ability to correct poverty and social dysfunction, radicals develop an ungodly hatred towards policy makers and so called religious leadership. The radical sees these individuals as hypocrites of the highest order. As a vocation, politics and sociology is where the radical brother butters his bread. In this case social science offers the requisite expression to work out his dissatisfaction with a system he believes is rooted in white supremacy

As I have mentioned throughout this writing process each prisoner type presents its own convoluted web. The Radical is no different. Emerging from the bowels of poverty, there are three Radical forms, each having an unparalleled placement inside a construct of social exclusion. I have termed these individuals the Pseudo-Radical, The Enemy of the State (EOTS), and the most active of the three, the Social Radical. All three operate with a mind toward social protest but the degree to which each position is demonstrated is a direct correlation to each prisoner's anarchist mindset. The most docile of this anarchist kind are the Pseudo-Radicals. They merely fringe protest and outrage but when their physical well-being is threatened as a result thereof, they retreat to a safe corner until the all-clear sign is given. Each type breaks down like this:

1. Pseudo-Radical: A social novice. Having an inclination toward radicalism but insufficient knowledge and life experience renders his efforts fruitless. His vocalizations propagate social reproof although his actions are of the nature of a coward who ducks physical confrontation or discomfort. Rhetoric of radicalism in this case is purely dramatic folly intent on deceiving on-lookers into believing he is principled, no nonsense, and a truth warrior, but the opposite is true. He is a vocal coward who uses emotionally charged words or rhetoric to hide his fear and pain of being incarcerated. His words are no more than a human form of barking.

2. The Enemy of the State (EOTS): These are the most dangerous Radical kind, even more dangerous than the master Criminal, in that EOTS by way of philosophical consecration has an inclination for state terrorism -- hence the term Enemy of the State. In contrast, MCs (Master Criminals) are isolated deviants who are mostly harmful to the communities from which they were plucked. Their (MCs') only desire is wealth accumulation and social relevance within their respective circle. For the EOTS every political or legal infraction upon the personage or community of blacks, Latinos, or poor whites only enhances his radical stance.

3. Social Radical (SR): He is what I call Propagated Purity, Consulate Leader, Prison Rights Activist. The SR lives each day in prison as if in preparation for the civic, social, and political stance he intends to take upon release. Prison serves as makeshift battlefield for future battles. SRs are the second most feared prison mind next to the Intellectuals.

It would normally be my practice to flesh-out each Radical via interview but in this regard I will only interview the EOTS due to his critical nature. I believe the definition for both Pseudo-Radical and Social Radical is sufficiently explained, although I might add that Pseudo-Radicals are inauthentic in their social relevance and therefore aren't worthy of acknowledgment. The idealism and views of the EOTS is put on full display.

Enemy of the State (The Interview)

Note: before the interview started I talked for about an hour with the EOTS about his character and how he fits within prison's overall scheme.

Q: Before we start, thank you for allowing me to interview you. In observing your type for some time now I know how you prefer operating from the shadows. You have my word to keep this interview anonymous, but I also expect you to fully open up and give the public a glimpse into your thinking. On that note what do think about my description of your kind?

EOTS: When I first heard you describe this EOTS character I honestly thought this dude is going too hard with this labeling shit. But after analyzing your terms on the various deviant characters I must confess you are 90% accurate in your assessment, though I disagree with the manner you chose to put this information out to the public at the expense of other prisoner types.

Q: Let's talk about that point for a minute. A few seconds ago you stated my description of the deviant individuals is 90% accurate, but yet you're saying now you disagree with the manner I've chosen to put these deviants on display. What is it about my actions you disagree with, if you care to explain?

EOTS: Well, you are the one who has made defining prisoner types your vocation, therefore I believe as a social observer you know my angle in the grand scheme of it all.

Q: Yes, I do have an idea why you said what you said, but for the purpose of this interview, allow me to put your thoughts, words and/or opinions on paper for those who might pick up this book. Please oblige me in this regards.

EOTS: OK, I'll give you what you want, regretfully so. I'll entertain you. Look man, I said what I said earlier because I am true to the character type you have poignantly defined as EOTS. Being a prisoner who possesses EOTS traits why would I want them people (Prison officials, FBI, CIA, etc.) who can hurt us (prisoners) having an inside track on our (prisoners') nature and/or thought process when I believe places like this are diabolically constructed to destroy black and brown lives?

I don't believe your book set out to work against us, nevertheless it has similar and unintended consequences. Look brother, when performing an act of war – and I know you understand prison to be an act of war against black and brown lives, so I won't insult your intelligence by attempting to explain that concept to you, I'm simply purporting no rational warrior reveal his faults and weaknesses to people or a system they intend to destroy. This is what you are essentially doing for prison officials in the chapters I was allowed to read. You, brother, are giving them an internal look into the depleted souls hidden from the public eyes. I compare your writing process to a 1940's country club allowing Negroes unfettered access. And whether for good or for bad, your detailed description on prison activity is more extensive than any article or book I've read on prisoners' conduct and condition. Truthfully I'm afraid your sociological observation as you call it will cause prison officials and society in particular to further turn on an already fucked-up man. It's like inside trading to me: instead of stock information you are divulging character stock to individuals who may use your book as legislative fodder against those incarcerated.

Q: I hear and respect your assumption brother, however the opposite side of the coin is true for my book premise. Unlike you, I see it as a project to promote prison reform by first allowing the public to peer inside prison walls, and secondly I thought by putting the various prison characters on display, prison officials would see their policy errors and how such policy helps to promote defiance. So never was it or is it my intent to act as some kind of insider prison snitch as your words kind of suggested.

Besides, how could someone such as myself having nearly twenty years invested in prison and prison issues be anything but an ally for prisoners and prison reform?

EOTS: Hold on Bro, forgive me if I made it sound as tho you are acting like an agent for the State, that's not what I was trying to do. I was attempting to convey that when your enemy knows your comings and goings, your strength and weaknesses, he's then able to exact pain and a plan to further destroy us. Your book in my opinion possesses all the qualities thereof – at least in that regards.

Q: Your statement is fair; I buy your logic but tell me this, why do your type seem to place all the blame for your ills on government and white people? And on that note, how much responsibility do we (prisoners and the communities they come from) hold for our wretched condition?

EOTS: You make it sound like I'm an all out lunatic all void of logic. It's just the way I see society. Historically we (black people) haven't had the political might nor unity to change society or even our own communities for the better. What I have witnessed more and more is black cultured died striving to be white, think white, and act white. The only thing white people accept that's black is the rhythms of our rhyme and songs through bass and snares, except for maybe acculturated white girls who desire big butts, lips, and tanned brown skin.

Q: I'm listening to your argument but find it rather out of sort and uncomfortable since you lump all white people in the same category, and it fails to take into account the changes blacks instigated by way of civil disobedience and the like. Wasn't the civil rights movement a form of political unity and empowerment for black people?

EOTS: In a way that's true, and you can still see the result of it but that's just it. It failed as an absolute model for wielding generational power or wealth. This is why we're more segregated, incarcerated and uneducated than when Dr. King was alive. I wonder what Dr. King would think now of his grand scheme of drinking and eating out of the same cups and plates of white folks without first establishing financial independence within the common ties we live. I bet he's rolling over in his grave watching the social and political actions of his pure white brothers.

Q: I'm gonna take it you're being a bit factious calling white people pure and a brother to Dr. King?

EOTS: Yeah I was, that clearly was a joke. In my opinion the only time black men can be true brothers to white folks is in death because decomposition in this way eliminate any potential harm to white supremacy. Dead black men become white folk heroes because they no longer pose a threat.

Q: Don't you think your language is a bit racist, essentially condemning all white people as racist?

EOTS: No, because every white person past and present has benefited from their white flesh. I don't hear them denouncing their white forefathers. Surely they won't do that because they still benefit from white patriarchy. You would think after centuries of humanitarian ills perpetuated by whites against others that they would relish an opportunity to denounce their white bodies and white privilege, but No! They thrive in a patriarchal system that continues to elevate them above all others.

Q: Boy, you said a lot. I agree with your assessment of white supremacy and /or white patriarchy but your views on white people as a whole I'll have to disagree strongly, although they are your views and you are entitled to them. Since we both agree white supremacy is alive and real, let's talk about how it looks and how do you purpose we do away with it.

EOTS: The structure huh? Well, look at it this way. Name all the civic, social, political and economic stations of society, and I bet you couldn't name one field where black folks are the creators and have the final say in decisions. You can't can you? Because there aren't any even in 2013.

Q: What about President Obama.

EOTS: What about him? I knew you were going there. Maybe you don't know this but Obama is not a black President. No matter how hard we make him out to be black Obama will for eternity be bi-racial. See that's what I'm talking about. We are so deficient of real examples of leadership in Black, we fall for anything. Obama don't even want to be associated with black people and his daughters look blacker than my own. Here's a man who does everything in his power not to utter the word black in his speeches and he has benefited from an overwhelming Black turnout. It's mind boggling how we (Black people) keep supporting folks who don't give a damn about us or our condition.

Q: Your point is well received. I have always held Obama as a bi-racial brother. In fact, Obama is the truest representation of America's melting pot so he doesn't just belong to Black people. And truthfully I believe it to be disrespectful to White Americans for blacks and ignorant whites to keep calling Obama a Black President. In my opinion, a Black President would look like Al Sharpton, Jessie Jackson and maybe Minister Louis Farrakhan. You know like I know, White Americans and some Black Americans would never vote for these individuals. Therefore Obama's bi-racial make-up is 50% responsible for his presidency. Talk about perfect timing, talk about things lining up. The Obama stuff is still emotional material so let's go to another topic. So what role should Government play in Black folk lives?

EOTS: The simple answer would be none, but I know you expect me to expound more on this. Look, I believe those in government are hypocrites and do more harm than good at the end of the day. Through Government our rights were given and through government our rights were taken. What am I saying? The civil rights movement was Government related and at the same time gentrification, deplorable schools, and economic disparity in urban centers are also Governmental. Back in the

112

50's and early 60's, before civil rights took hold black folks did for themselves. We were forced to. We owned a number of businesses and were responsible for educating our own children. After civil rights one can legitimately argue we are worse off and more in need of governmental assistance than ever before. Notwithstanding DCFS and other similar agencies now tell us how to rear our children or they will take them from us. Man I welcome the opportunity to help bring down Government.

Q: Say more about that. When you say bring down Government, what do you mean by it?

EOTS: It's clear- you're not stupid. I mean to destroy it by any means necessary.

Q: Alright, I think I understand your angle. Tell me then, what are your feelings regarding the 9/11 attack in New York.

EOTS: That was the greatest joy of my life next to sex. To see such a wicked nation receiving a dose of its own medicine is therapeutic. It felt so good watching such a universal bully being brought low to its knees. Man, I smiled all day long. I never got enough of watching those planes slam into the towers.

Q: But brother, the Government wasn't the only ones affected by 9/11's terrorist act. Innocent people died in those towers.

EOTS: Get that soft shit out of my face Bro. No one is innocent who is tied to a modern day imperialist. This is a warlord nation man. Those individuals were casualties of war – how is it any different from America and Israel killing Arab women and children while cowardly launching missiles from the air and sea at suspected terrorists? American citizens have no way of knowing if they were or were not terrorist. We just have to take the military's word for it. So try that innocent shit on someone who gives a fuck! I don't.

Q: Wow, Bro. Do you really believe no one is innocent in matters of war?

EOTS: Yes, I do.

Q: OK. What about the terrorists' methods for exacting punishment in war?

EOTS: It doesn't matter how war gets done, just that it's effective, and believe me, their (terrorist) methods are very effective. Look at how America responds to terrorist tactics, even breaking "Geneva Convention" rules when executing war. Americans even launch missiles over other countries without permission or due process. We still support Israel's excessive bombing of Palestine and Hamas leadership don't we? Not to mention the cost in billions to tax payers. And finally look at us sitting here rotting away in prison without any help from those outside these walls. More than anyone you shouldn't even be here but you are. And they (FBI, CIA, etc.) wonder why we become enemy combatants like ole boy Jose Padilla, and white cats like Adam Adan. I have absolutely no sympathy for a nation who abandons its own and then expect us (prisoners) to not be affected by prison life with no supervision.

Q: You make a strong and scary argument. My final question is, if given an opportunity would you take up arms against America?

EOTS: All that's easy. Yes! Not only would I take up arms but if I thought I could get away with it I would help groups like Al Qaeda blow up America.

Q: Are you serious?!

EOTS: I'm more serious than the 25 years I've been in prison.

Q: Thank you for your candor. I appreciate you trusting me with your views. When the FBI and CIA read this you and I are both going to Gitmo. (smile)

EOTS: No problem, remember this interview never happened (smile).

114

Q: What interview? (smile).

In case it hasn't registered, the EOTS' ideological framework is more dangerous and more centralized than any other MC operating in prison. The EOTS may or may not come to a point of reconciliation while in prison; the prison situation certainly does nothing to dispel the EOTS' perceptions. That's why it's imperative for courts and prison houses to stay out front on reform policies. Men like these can't be left alone in dark cell corners adopting terrorist concepts out of anger for a system he perceives as unjust or simply out of being bored. Incentives must be put in place which encourage and reward good behavior, for not doing so indicates an acceptance of prison as potential terrorist producing dens. Therefore I have found that incarceration only increases terrorist mind states. Moral and intellectual stagnation create ripe bodies for resentment and revenge; poor communities are the first to experience the wrath of EOTS types. Am I'm the only person who sees this? Am I the only one who cares? I truly hope not.

Chapter 9: Prison Hustler (PH)

A Hustler's Creed

"Uh Nixxx ain't gon' be hungry fo' nobody. In this world the only thing movin' is money and I'm ma get mine by any means necessary even if it mean body bagging uh Nixxx to get it. I don't give a damn what people think, I'm going after mine. I betcha I ain't gon' be starving, broke, wit my hand out begging nobody for nothing. Hustling is all uh Nixxx know how to do. All my life I've been poe! It ain't no fun wearing hand me downs. Uh Nixxx having shit is the only thing people respect and I'm gettin' my respect, jus' watch me."

Throughout urban America, poverty and what's perceived as American exceptionalism play a major part in influencing the above mind set. Hailing from communities of disadvantage myself I am sympathetic to the material grind of Prison Hustlers but what I take issue with is the fact most PH's never graduate from petty hustling into grander entrepreneurial endeavors even when they possess the requisite ability to do so. In this instance it appears PH types have no will or desire to divorce themselves from underground monetary pursuits in exchange for legally binding ones.

In homes where poverty is inescapable young boys find economic and manhood examples from Rap music, reality shows and in the consummate neighborhood pharmacist/drug dealer. These characters shape and mold young boys in ways that are life altering and lead to a kind of social construct centered around acquiring "green paper" over integrity. PH's are therefore made or *unmade* in impoverished households long before they enter prison where destructive behaviors are acted out for the duration of their sentence. Everything is about capital and capitalism for the PH. It's the only thing that's real, although his limited working knowledge of capitalism put him at odds not only with the legal system but also the communities he hustles in.

A Hustler's Narrative

It is 1983. Every day after school Darnell heads over to his neighborhood grocery store where he carries old ladies' grocery bags for change. He never understood the pure sense of capitalism at 14. What is evident though is his understanding of the value in services. For 3 months, like the mechanism in a fine Swiss watch, he became a persistent fixture of hustle in the store parking lot. The funny thing about this apparent entrepreneurial wherewithal is that no one paid Darnell any mind. A thousand individuals passed him by each day, never once bothering to have a conversation as to why he hustled grocery bags or about his entrepreneurial ingenuity. Neighborhood police rolled by without saying a word even though Darnell was violating peddling laws. I guess it's safe to assume law enforcement deems this a harmless act and figured as long as this knucklehead is doing something positive he's not their concern. But is what Darnell is doing truly positive or is it a prelude towards elevated criminal behavior? And why wouldn't it be a problem when Darnell's hustling violated state rules for proper execution of trade and commerce? For that matter, does Darnell even know what an article of incorporation or peddler's license is given his socioeconomic background? Since no one says anything to him he feels within his right to hustle bags for nickels and dimes.

There he works to save enough money to cop two pounds of weed he intends to distribute throughout the hood. Don't be surprised by this revelation. What did you think would come out of this? The question should be where did Darnell get the idea to convert grocery store change into a drug enterprise?[21]

There's no need to remind Darnell about the irrationality of such an undertaking today; with hindsight even the ignorant are made wise. But at 14, with ghetto surroundings as his primary

---

[21] This account is based on a true story. When I was younger I personally witnessed a couple of neighborhood kids turn parking lot change into a $12 - $15,000 a day drug empire. I often wonder who taught them this or what type of mindset boys like these must have to think in this way? Hustling or Entrepreneurship is clearly a natural talent.

teacher, hustling to purchase weed is a type of success that only increase Darnell's haughtiness! Very rarely in such an environment does anyone succeed at anything. Darnell's discipline to save up nickels and dimes to purchase drugs is a moral victory he saw up close and personal. Although his activity of hustling grocery bags to purchase drugs is shortsighted.

Someone living in the suburbs or who has always held a lofty station in life would dare to criticize Darnell's behavior without first analyzing all the life variables nurturing such dysfunction. A self-righteous air forms quite often from an 'us against them' idealism that unfairly places total blame on the teenager for his underground economic pursuit. People make judgment without ever considering the economic depression of these environments. It's an action I describe as 'the hen asking an egg why it wants to be a rooster'. Darnell's behavior represent the absurdity of Capitalism and the drunken irrationality of entrepreneurship.

Let's consider another thought for a second. Here we have a 14 year old kid with the work ethic to earn coins as a stepping stone towards what we now know to be underground supply and demand but capitalism nonetheless. While in pursuit of what could be deemed the American Dream no one offers Darnell encouragement. No one advises him on economic principles or rules governing commerce e.g. taxes, stocks, bonds, etc. For that matter, Darnell has never heard of Adam Smith or of his capitalistic philosophy; and how would he come by such knowledge when the public school he attended never taught him about Adam Smith? This was the case for me. It wasn't until maybe my senior year in high school that I recall reading about Adam Smith's capitalist philosophy.

The fact remains everyone passes by this kid of promise without imparting an ounce of financial wisdom on him, all passer-by offer is criticism and judgment. His ability to use labor to acquire change is uniquely American, but no one notices. With no economic guidance, ghetto dwellers like

Darnell learn improper life and monetary skills observing gang bangers, drug dealers and pimps while every citizen passes by Darnell without giving him one word of encouragement. There are 10 street hustlers who welcome the opportunity to steer him in the wrong direction. Subsequently two pounds of weed turn into five, five turn to ten, and over the course of 3 to 6 years Darnell becomes bait for the criminal justice system. Although Hustlers come in all forms, Darnell's story advances my narrative of the Hustler's beginnings.

A PH LIFE

The PH character spans from average to complex depending on street hustling experience. The most successful prisoners are those receiving social and financial support from the outside via family and friends. Outside support is critical given most prisoners receive a state stipend of $10-15 dollars each month to purchase hygienic and other personal items. Understand that like society inflation affects prisoners as well. It takes on average $25-$30 a month to purchase soap, toothpaste, detergent, deodorant, lotion, shampoo and hair oil from the prison commissary. Prisoners receiving only $15 a month with no outside support are placed at a hygienic disadvantage. Purchasing things like new underwear, t-shirts thermal, socks and other clothing items is out of the question. What's a prisoner to do for survival except hustle?

The public believes we live comfortable lives in prison, but the truth is with the ever increasing budgetary problems throughout the country, the first group to feel the financial sting from cut backs are public schools and prisoners. Our (prisoners) food allotment grows more limited and nutritionally deficient, therefore to compensate for dietary deficiencies prisoners purchase vitamins ($5.00) and other food items from commissary – that being those prisoners who can afford commissary. Most goods sold on commissary are 2 or 3 times higher than items sold in society, 'outside'. The extra-ordinary financial tariff placed on prison goods is so inhumane that a number of organizations have sought judicial redress to reduce prison commissary prices. In the meantime what's a prisoner to do but hustle to overcome prison's monopoly when no outside financial support is forthcoming? The proceeding section details the PH's method and daily grind for surviving his prison digs.

The Method and the Madness

In order to gain a financial stronghold it is not uncommon for PH's to take on similar habits as those of the preceding character, The Liar. The average PH uses deception and lies to solidify his scheme, where the more sophisticated PH's rely on skill and the gift of gab to obtain his material ends. His methods are out front and transparent, he skillfully disarms his victims. The comparison below provides an example of two extremes within the PH category:

Low Level/Average Hustler	Complex Hustler
1. Compromised Integrity	1. High Integrity
2. Will lie to achieve ends	2. Achieves ends through honesty and transparency
3. Will steal from anyone to achieve ends	3. Sees stealing from other prisoners as a weak character trait; will only steal from prison officials
4. Won't seek employment to earn a living	4. Will seek employment to earn a living
5. Doesn't see begging as shameful	5. Sees begging as shameful
6. Doesn't mind reputation taking a hit	6. A good reputation is central to mystique

Low Level/Average Hustler	Complex Hustler
7. Will turn prison informant to receive material favors	7. Won't sell out to receive material favors.

Tools and Access

Every apprentice or journeyman use tools in his chosen profession. It is no less the case for PHs. As stated in the previous section, average and complex hustlers use the gift of gab as a primary tool to soften up his victim en route to separate them from their material goods. In the prison world those goods are commissary items such as soap, toothpaste, deodorant, meat packs (sardines, tuna, chili, etc.), sweets, chips, and sometimes clothing and gym shoes. To achieve their commissary end every hustler must have access to prison areas where inaccessible items are located, stolen, and then traded for accessible items (commissary goods). Below are three columns detailing the PH's tools, access and inaccessible items.

Tools/Skills	Access – prison work areas and/or victim proximity	Inaccessible items – things which can't be bought at commissary
Lying, cheating, stealing Card games: spades, poker, casino Shooting craps Chess Running a store Drawing portraits Arts & Crafts	Kitchen worker (site of most inaccessible food items Clinical service worker – source of copies, whiteout, tape, office supplies Officer commissary worker Institutional laundry worker	Fruits Vegetables – onions, green peppers, tomatoes, etc. Spices Sugar, honey, syrup, jams Bread, & grains – oatmeal, grits, rice Butter and oils –

Tools/Skills	Access – prison work areas and/or victim proximity	Inaccessible items – things which can't be bought at commissary
(greetings cards, watchbands, key chain, etc.)	Cell house laundry porter	actually margarine; real butter is not used
Repair clothing w/ sewing kit	Gym worker	Milk
Writing poetry	Cell house porter	Fish, chicken, eggs
	Institutional tailor shop	Cheese
	Teacher's aide	Condiments
Writing love letters for prisoners	Hub porter (prison guard work area)	Scotch tape, electrical tape
(also done by Prison Players)	Inside grounds (picking up trash, etc. inside prison grounds)	Office supplies – whiteout, paper clips, rubber bands (erasers)
Write college essays and papers for fellow prisoners. Intellectuals can make $ this way.	Outside grounds – movement beyond prison gates	Cleaning supplies & chemicals
Gambling on sports	Maintenance worker (electrician, plumber)	Weekly call to the barber
Electronic repair (head phones, radio, etc.)	Barber shop worker	Ace bandages, alcohol pads, aspirin, pain pills
Barbering skills (hair braiding)	Hospital worker	New prison blues, sheets, pillow cases, boots, coats
	Clothing room worker	Extra copies, legal materials, typewriter use, legal book check-out
	Library clerk	

A Prelude to Hustling

Each day for the PH is a day spent preoccupied with gaining access to accessible and inaccessible items located throughout prison. No pursuit is the same; each is met with its own set of challenges that can prove profitable or lead to a temporary stay in segregation if caught stealing or in possession of inaccessible merchandise. For this section, I will only highlight the hustling activity of The Merchant, The Gambler, and The Kitchen Thief, but before I elaborate on these three characters the following is a list of Hustlers we'll not talk about:

1. The Eclectic – The Artist: Charges $1 to $50 for Art work and other craft work.

2. The Electrician: Charges $3 to $5 to repair electronics, like radios, TV's and head phones.

3. The Runner: Usually porters with an expanded reach who carry merchandise from cell house to cell house. They charge $1 to $5 for trafficking merchandise throughout prison.

4. Porters: Makes cell to cell, deck to deck moves for prisoners that add up to future favors.

5. The Tailor: Charges $1 to $5 to sew items by hand.

6. Laundry Porter: Charges $2 or more monthly to wash certain prisoners clothes; he also makes cell to cell transactions for a fee.

7. The Pill Peddler: Sells medication: Aspirin, pain pills, and even psych meds for accessible items.

8. The Jail House Lawyer: Charges anywhere from $5 to $100 to prepare legal motions and briefs, will expound more on this character in Chapter 10.

9. The Clothing Room Worker: Sells stolen state blues, t-shirts, boxers, and socks.

10. The Health Care Worker: Steals and sells inaccessible items from health care: ace bandages, cleaning chemicals, alcohol pads, ointments, pills, etc.

11. The Barber: Cuts hair and shaves prisoner for $2.

12. The Hair Braider: Charges $2 to braid hair.

13. The Teacher's Aide: Steals school supplies to trade for accessible items.

PH-3 The Merchant, The Gambler, The Kitchen Thief

If any prisoner were to wear the title entrepreneur it would be the one I classify as The Merchant. Every waking day for this individual is a day spent acquiring and selling accessible and inaccessible goods. His entire prison stint revolves around bartering and trading, even when all prison activity ceases due to lock-down. The Merchant can be found yelling down prison galleries like a skilled auctioneer fencing wares. When a sale is made he uses cell house porters for cell to cell transactions similar to a business using UPS and Fed Ex to deliver packages. The PH is an entrepreneurial marvel to behold; he increases his prison coffers with 3 entrepreneurial maneuvers known as:

1. The 2 for 1 hustle

2. Trade and traffic

3. The sugar and salt peddle.

The 2 for 1 Hustle

The 2 for 1 hustle functions just as it sounds. It is the oldest most lucrative hustling game employed by prisoners. A PH uses usury tactics to fill his prison issued storage box with commissary items and when there's no longer room to store his excess he rents out storage boxes of less fortunate prisoners. This begs the question: Who are the victims of the 2 for 1 hustle? Most often they are prisoners who rarely receive financial assistant from beyond prison via family and friends. They are individuals reliant upon menial prison jobs paying $15 to $28 a month; those prisoners unable to work due to inadequate ABE/GED qualification and all other prisoners receiving a $10 monthly institutional/utility stipend for hygienic needs. [22] Those prisoners receiving no outside support are considered impoverished and the perfect victim of merchant types.

The 2 for 1 hustle works like this. The PH receives two back in return, a form of loan sharking with a 100% profit margin. Less fortunate and financial irresponsible prisoners serve their entire sentence under 2 for 1 obligation to merchants. The PH traps his newest victim with patience and extreme kindness in order to milk his new victim like a cow. He reels him in like a fish on a hook with free merchandise. Purchasing thermal underwear, pajamas, and sweat suits is out of the question on a $10 state budget.

Sensing his victim's desperation the Merchant offers the following explanation: "Man, I don't have it to spare like that, I don't receive nothing from my family so I have to juggle the few items I got to survive but what I can do is let you have it until State pay but I'm gonna need two back in return for waiting on my Merchandise." "No problem, I'll give you two back."

Unless 2 for 1 victims possess special talents (i.e. Artist, hair braiding, barbering, etc.), they find themselves in an ever expanding hole of debt because of their inability to do without

---

22 Prison Commissary hygiene product breakdown (Illinois prisoners aren't given hygiene products for personal care, as may or may not happen in other states):
Soap $1.00 a bar
Detergent $3.00
Deodorant $3.00 generic $6.00 name brand
Hair food $5.00
Lotion $1- $4
Shampoo $2 - $5
Toothpaste $2 - $4
T-shirts $5 a piece
Boxers $15
Socks $1- 2 a pair

by living within their means. By the time 2 for 1 victims wake up to the 2 for 1 hustle, hundreds have been wasted. Then it's on to the next undisciplined sucker. The Merchant will exploit prisoners like these his whole prison bid. Having used prison as a base for honing his exploitive tactics, Merchants like these become future drug dealers in urban communities upon release. A cycle of exploitation continues until permanent imprisonment or death, although even then there's always someone willing to step into The Merchant's void.

The Trade and Traffic (TNT)

In here the term "Trade" means the accessible and inaccessible goods that are available for bartering services are traded as well. To "Traffic" simply means the mode by which available goods are transported or handed over. Hand to hand, prisoner to prisoner transportation is the most common method to traffic goods when in close proximity. When goods are to be traded or exchanged from one cell house to another, those with movement such as Porters, inside/outside ground workers, and those having access to the Educational building can be used as traffickers. This method is also used to transport gang literature throughout prison.

In an effort to curtail Trade and Traffic Prison Administrators institute anti-trade and traffic rules, violation of said rules can lead to lost privileges, loss of good time credit, and ultimately time in segregation. T-N-T is the single most administrative rule every prisoner violates regardless of class, type or timidity. T-N-T is a necessary evil for any prisoner seeking not only to survive his confines but to acquire those material good he deems would provide a sense of comfort while in hell. Those in a position to traffic goods are highly regarded prisoners.

The Sugar and Salt Peddle

In prison just like in society prisoners look for ways to cope with the stresses of life, in this case those stresses produced by a life determined by concrete and steel. Similar to society prisoners mask their confinement by ingesting into their bodies substances that will help then escape reality. Prisoners use fake psychological issues in order to be prescribed psych meds due to their potent nature. Sex and drugs are difficult to obtain unless you fit into a particular caste or possess a level of financial stability that allow sex and drugs to be purchased from prison staff. Since sex and drugs aren't readily available, the majority of prisoners rely on the cheapest, oldest, most obtainable stress reducer available for consumption; sugar and salt.

It should come as no surprise, 1 out of 4 prisoners has diabetes and high blood pressure. Sugar and salt peddlers push cookies, candy, and chips like drugs. They understand the addictive properties in cookies and chips and thus use them as tools for exploitation and usury. Like a lonely woman camped out on her sofa with a box of her favorite chocolate to escape the pain of a lost love, nothing works like cookies and chips to soothe the pain of confinement. When prisoners run out of their sugar and salt supply the sugar and salt peddler store is always open. At any given time he may have two or three prisoners storing merchandise in their prison issued storage box that he rents for $3 - $5 monthly, or the prisoner is paid with sweet and salty goods himself.

In addition sugar and salt peddlers increase their profit margins by manufacturing lollipop type candy from Kool-Aid, jolly ranchers, lemonheads or any combination of chocolate and peanuts that they then sell for 25 and 50 cents. By creating 25 cent sugary treats they are able to profit even from less fortunate prisoners. These 25 cents lollipops are also given out on credit to be paid on state pay. No one escapes the capitalistic grasp of sugar and salt peddlers. If there's a will they will find a way to get in every prisoner's pocket even if it means giving away free lollipops to sugar and salt suckers (pun intended).

The Gambler

There is none more independent than The Gambler. He will not be found moping around complaining about not receiving financial support from outside. He takes pride in making things happen, not waiting for things to happen to and for him. His entire prison bid is regulated by gambling, he gambles not only for financial gain but also as a type of psycho-social distraction from his prison existence. But in the end gambling for him is about winning. He finds pleasure in dominating another through gambling, money and/or commissary items are simply by-products of successful domination. Gambling is his culture, his life.

It should come as no surprise that narcissism and arrogance are inherent traits in all prisoners. For the gambler these character defects are enhanced. In free society gambling for this particular prisoner was a secondary occupation next to selling drugs, committing robberies and other forms of crime to acquiring funds. Only after entering prison does gambling take on this hyper form due to primary occupational void. As a psycho-social mechanism for overcoming prison boredom gambling is exercised through the following media:

1. Dice
2. Cards (spades, poker, casino)
3. Betting on sports (basketball, football, baseball). All other sports activities fall in separate categories other than the three above.
4. Horse Racing
5. NASCAR
6. Hockey
7. Prison sports tournaments
8. Chess
9. Knowledge and information (This simply means when there's a dispute about knowledge or information, prisoners bet on whose knowledge or information is more accurate).

The Kitchen Thief (KT)

The kitchen is where most "inaccessible items" are located and no prisoner is better at obtaining inaccessible items than the KT. Earlier I provided a list of inaccessible items therefore it isn't necessary to repeat it. All inaccessible items come through the hands of KTs. They are essential to serving time since food is the cornerstone of life. In prison having a good KT in your circle makes for a comfortable stay. Food may or may not remove the sting of imprisonment but it's the next best thing to sex and freedom. It's all we have.

Chapter 10: The Jail House Lawyer (JHL)

In an environment where faith, hope, and perseverance are deflated notions, the Jailhouse Lawyers embody all three qualities. Their power of will to push towards freedom long after the criminal court process has beat down other prisoners is a testament to an inner strength that supersedes his reality. Anyone who has ever gone through pre-conviction stages of the criminal "just-us" system knows the tedious aspect of being ushered back and forth from cell house to courthouse until eventually being brought to submission via conviction or the ever popular proposition of a plea bargain. The plea bargain is a pressure induced proposition which entangles 80 to 90 percent of minorities entering American Court houses, and 95-97% of all cases. Jails and prisons are therefore revolving doors of degradation that continue to degrade long after the sentence is over.

Not so for the JHL. He is a consummate fighter who never gives in even when evidence strongly suggests he should. A plea deal or copping out means living to fight another day for the average prisoner, but copping out for JHLs mean permissive and passive death in a box. Observing JHLs for some time now I often wonder where do these apparent legal novices develop such legal resolve and research readiness during their confinement, while apparently falling short in exercising these same attributes pre-conviction or post release. I'm puzzled by this discovery because it's clear they possess the requisite skills to have been great attorneys. Watching these men in the prison law library put together legal motions, briefs and petitions is an action at top law firms. Every day is spent researching case law and petitioning the court to recognize the many constitutional violations throughout his or other prisoners criminal proceedings. They are the last bastion of hope standing between hopelessness and freedom, they are the gatekeepers of prison appeals. Similar to proceeding types JHLs fall into 3 hierarchical categories: The Real, The Fake, and The Hustler.

The Real JHLR

The Real is just what it implies. JHLRs are the most knowledgeable paralegal types. The study of law and/or jurisprudence is second nature to him. His character screams "look I'm an attorney not a prisoner." JHLRs are even more beloved than intellectuals for the service they lend to fellow prisoners. The following points put the JHLR's relevance in greater context:

- They act, think, and breath law and all that it entails.

- They tend to work or spend the bulk of their leisure time in the prison library researching case law and helping others work on appeals. No single activity is more important to this type.

- Where other prisoners are talking sports, politics and religion JHLRs are found conversing and philosophizing about legal statutes.

- Of the 3 JHLs, JHLRs are the most altruistic. In matters of law they will entertain any question no matter friend or foe.

- Confusing legal precedence rarely frustrate the JHLR. No legal issue is too heavy for him to tackle. If there's case law available offering legal precedence for the issue at hand he will find it.

- Law is his social, political and spiritual escape.

- His bible is his law books and the words therein is synonymous with the word of God.

- They respect the language of law and study legal jargon as a pass-time.

- JHLRs spend all disposable funds on legal materials. Their property boxes are filled with legal books, case law, and legal newsletters. When they run out of space to store excess legal materials they then pay or persuade other prisoners to hold legal excess.

- JHLRs rarely seek a fee for helping prisoners with legal petitions and briefs, they see it as an obligation. If charity is exchanged they accept it but rarely solicit fees.

- JHLF and JHLH seek out JHLRs for legal advice.

- JHLRs file merit based petitions that are accepted by the courts.

- They are relentless litigators; prison officials tread lightly around these individuals for fear of being sued.

- They win a number of institutional related lawsuits before they are released.

- JHLRs have been known to have thousands of dollars in their prison accounts from suing the institution. Because they have their own money they tend not to rely on outside financial support. Some JHLRs write checks and help pay bills from prison.

- JHLRs are men serving 20 years to life; one third of that time will be spent in prison libraries and by happenstance a high legal IQ is developed overtime.

- They watch all things legal on television' especially boring trials, HLN type programs are their favorite.

- JHLRs have been known to enter into intimate relationships with female lawyers from top law firms due to their talent and charisma.

- JHLRs are often solicited by law firms to work as paralegals upon release.

The Fake (JHLF)

The fakes are also knowledgeable in matters of law but their lazy unfocused nature prevents them from fully committing to legal research; and their impatience prevents them from becoming students of law. They see law as a means to an end and not a way of life as the proceeding points will show:

- Law is a pastime, a means to an end.

- They use the prison library to escape their confines and for linking up with likeminded individuals.

- JHLF only converses about law when it's conducive to his goal or project.

- They study law for the purpose of filing some kind of civil suit against prison administrations. Law is about creating a civil pay day, they rarely talk law unless it involves money. Law is more like a radical affront to prison administrations as opposed to a legal necessity.

- The legal process frustrates the JHLF.

- They believe every case filed is merit based and unassailable. He often overlooks precedent setting cases as a result of research laziness. His legal briefs are peppered with the frivolity of misplaced vitriol.

The Hustler (JHLH)

The Hustler is the least knowledgeable in the JHL hierarchy. He is a legal bottom feeder who feeds off prisoner's hopes of obtaining freedom through the appeals process. Every man entering prison who was assigned a public defender believes he was under represented. It's understandable. I had a paid attorney and felt that way. With that being the case JHLHs play on these emotions by using the hope of appeal to exploit prisoners financially. He makes his living filing petitions and briefs he knows won't stand up to the light of day. The JHLHs' legal activity and thought process are as follows:

- Has only a basic knowledge of law though his legal jargon is quite impressive.

- Uses legal jargon and the gift of gab to trap vulnerable prisoners into his legal web.

- As with to the Fake, law is a means to an end where the only purpose for delving into legal issue is to obtain financial independence.

- A JHLH uses the expertise of JHLRs to prepare legal petitions for other prisoners then charges a fee to the prisoner for work he didn't do.

- He uses the prison library to meet up with homies and fellow gang members.

- Where JHLFs use the law to file civil suits against prison admin, the JHLH uses it to hustle commissary items by filing a bunch of frivolous petitions he knows won't move the court to act.

- He never misses an opportunity to "discuss" legal issues with fellow prisoners since law is his instrument for exploitation.

- Unlike JHLF, the JHLH is extremely patient with the legal process because it is his business, although he doesn't believe in the legal process himself. He inspires his victims to believe in the law. Whether the case has merit or not isn't his concern. The more frivolous petitions he's able to file, the more commissary he can collect.

- The JHLH lies to his victims about the merit of their legal issues and when their petitions are denied by the court he then blames the Judge for not following case law.

- In prison hierarchy JHLHs live pretty well as a result of their legal exploits.

In conclusion, prison houses are filled with competent legal minds that use legal angles to create justice for the prison population and themselves but as evident by the JHL hierarchy there are those who use legal skill for exploitive ends. Where exploitation is a normal aspect of prison culture, no act of exploitation generates emotions like those with implications of freedom attached to them. Serving a prison sentence is the ultimate equalizer that prisoners of every type and kind seek to get out from under, so it's not illogical for freedom starved men to fall prey to the trick of freedom's possibility.

Chapter 11: The Intellectual/ Philosopher

A Reflective Cell

In my cell dwelling I often imagine a world free from social constructs characterized by hiding behind religion and patriotism while practicing something entirely contradictory in private. I further imagine a society where justice and fair-play outweigh classism and political maneuvering, where the content of one's character truly outpaces patriarchy structures which have for so long defined the rules and standards as to how humanity should look, think, and behave.

From my prison cell I reflect on the internal complexities of my biological makeup: A complexity of cells that are unapparent to the cell walls holding my body from freedom. I likewise reflect on the power biology has on my ability to endure the pressure of confinement. From the outside, prisons are viewed as punishment for an infraction committed against the public, but to me it's more transformative. In a world where freedom of movement is more valuable than freedom of mind I contend that my prison cell is organically suited to align mind and spirit to my cellular being, therefore my primary concern is the qualitative development associated with prison space and time continuum. Henceforth until release my cell and cell block represent a space where I plot excellence in every aspect of living going forward.

Alpha – Inception

It should come as no surprise Intellectual types are supreme in overall stratification. This is not because they deem themselves supreme, but because of their mental wherewithal to use prison's limited space and time for the acquisition of knowledge, discipline and spiritual insight – a brand of learning that brings into question the knowledge of God, self and other, and how spirit and flesh are intrinsically woven together. Becoming an Intellectual is a painstaking process. Lower tier prisoners/deviants are too lazy and immoral to cultivate without outside forces pressing up against their slack existence. For this reason prisoners possessing self-imposed wills like Intellectuals make them the most dangerous prisoners roaming prison grounds. Prison officials perform best when dealing with ignorant unsophisticated prisoners who expect nothing of themselves or of the correctional staff given charge over their confined bodies.

Not so for the Intellectual. He not only holds himself accountable but prison staff and administrators as well. The number of ethical violations that may go over the heads of average prisoners won't cut the mustard with Intellectuals. Intellects are proficient in both staff and prisoners rules. Whenever an incident arises where a staff member has acted outside ethical guidelines, intellectuals welcome the opportunity to address the matter through the grievance and the court of law, if necessary. It should come as no surprise that the grievance procedure for prisoners is broken as shown in previous chapters, nevertheless the grievance process is the first line of defense before the court is compelled to step in. Although it is a long and tedious process designed to frustrate justice, it nevertheless must be performed. The following 11 points offer insight into the workings of the grievance procedure:

1. When there's an issue in question the prisoner obtains a grievance form from the counselor or cell house CO's.

2. The standard grievance form is then filled out jotting down the prisoner's account of the incident he deems to be in violation of IDOC rules.

3. After this the grievance is given to the cell house counselor to investigate by questioning or bringing prisoner's concerns to the staff member the grievance was written on. [23]

4. The prisoner receives his grievance back from the counselor anywhere after 30 days to 3 months with his

---

[23] It's really more like a process of "snitching" on the prisoner to fellow staff members about the prisoner's complaint against them. At this stage it's a makeshift procedure since the officer will just deny the ethical infraction alleged by the prisoner.

or her response written in the area designated for response.[24]

5. The next stage is to send grievance with counselor response to a grievance officer who picks up where the counselor left off, by interviewing the officer with the same set of facts.[25]

6. Grievance officer returns grievance back to prisoner with similar response as the counselor before him or her except this time the response is presented in typed form to be kept in the record. Like the counselor before him the issue is rubber stamped and read "Prisoner claim is unsubstantiated.

7. Next stage is to send the grievance with the counselor's and grievance officer's response to the Warden for review.

8. Prisoner receives grievance back from the Warden 3 months or so later with a response that reads "I concur with the grievance officer that the issue is unsubstantiated and no further investigation is necessary. Grievance dismissed."

9. Unsatisfied with the Warden's ruling the next step is to send the grievance to the group overseeing prison operation in Springfield, Illinois, called the Administrator Review Board (ARB) for further review of issues.

10. 6 months or more later the grievance is returned from ARB stating the same as prisoner's institution saying: "I concur the matter was properly handled on the institutional level and nothing further will be done on this issue."

---

24 99% of the time the counselor's response is rubber stamped and read as "Unsubstantiated- the CO's states no such thing occurred" or "He doesn't recall the incident in question."

25 Even after providing witnesses to the counselor and the grievance officer as is permissible by prison grievance procedure, witnesses are rarely called to corroborate prisoner's claim.

11. The only other recourse after going through the prison "Kangaroo Court" process is to file a federal lawsuit to address the number of due process violations or whatever rules apply for filing a federal 1983 petition.

Why is highlighting these 11 points necessary? I wanted to show the level of resilience and moral fortitude prisoners must possess to even bother pursuing a grievance procedure that's deflating and defeated long before it was ever started. Without the institution of an independent grievance procedure separate and apart from the facilities holding prisoners bodies, addressing prisoners issues is clearly a foregone conclusion. Apart from JHLs and Intellectuals average prisoners are immediately frustrated with the process of pursuing justice. Even when a clear ethical violation has occurred demanding outside humanitarian attention, the grievance process is just to demeaning and stressful to pursue. This means COs get away with ethical infractions any other professionals would be suspended or fired for in free society. For this reason Intellectuals pose the greatest threat to the establishments of prison for having the resolve to pursue violations against prisoners all the way to court. Prison officials shun any and all legal and political heat which can arise from staff misconduct.

Incarceration and the Psyche of Confinement

As mentioned in earlier chapters individuals incarcerated for 10 years or more become preoccupied with character building that often develops into obsessive compulsive disorders that bleed into other areas of life. Some issues are open and apparent, while others are subtle, requiring psychological astuteness to detect. The following points illustrate many issues affecting Intellectuals who have served 10 years or more:

• Intellectuals are extreme narcissists who have come to discovering their potential due to time. Prison has afforded the Intellectual a long period to reflect on the ideas of God, self, and others.

- Intellectuals are self-righteous moralists. I know, I've been called that on a number of occasions.

- Wears his Intelligence on his sleeves. Years of studying has given him a plethora of knowledge; he thinks his intellect is superior to all others except for those scholars and critical thinkers whose writings shape his concepts and idealism.

- Collects and hoards intellectual material even when he knows there's no room to store it.

- Intellectuals often use grandiloquent jargon to make a simple point.

- Is often never wrong and stands firm in his knowledge until serious refutation is put forth compelling him to move beyond prior knowledge.

- Functions from logic, the more knowledge he obtains, the less this type believes in God.

- Possesses an obsessive body and mind image of himself.

- Overly concerned with how he's perceived by those around him.

- Believes the acquisition of knowledge ought to make perfect mind, body and behavioral sense and therefore see mistakes and errors as unacceptable; which further suggest he's too hard on himself and takes himself too seriously.

  Note: I know this to be true for me, I'm extremely hard on myself and take almost everything too serious. I'm working on this flaw but when you have wasted half of your life in a cell your present and future must be taken seriously. In this case who has time for games?

- His dreams, ideas, and entrepreneurial endeavors are exceptionally grand. Not that anything is wrong with having grand ideas but with sentences ranging from 40 years to life maybe time could be better spent surviving the rigors of prison.

- Can be over bearing and extremely possessive.

- Has a number of annoying OCD issues that sometimes affect social life.

- Doesn't keep cell mates very long and when he does his living dynamic is quite contentious, stressful, and dominate shared living space.

- Very argumentative. Thinks every issue is up for debate.

Incarceration and the Psychology of Excellence

Now it would be unfair to put forth all the intellectual's overbearing traits without also highlighting his honorable and good ones. They are:

- An intense love for reading.

- Acquiring information and knowledge is second only to breathing. His vocation is studying.

- He writes daily. He loves the use of the pen.

- He questions everything, debates issues for entertainment purposes.

- He makes no excuse for failures, failure is a weakness that occurs from not trying.

- He is culturally sound and loves his people.

- He loves politics, and is heavily invested in current events and world affairs.

- He enjoys helping other prisoners with incarceration and manhood identity issues.

- He serves as a mentor for younger prisoners, tutors them for ABE and GED testing.

- Intellectuals possess impeccable manners, and show the utmost respect to fellow prisoners and staff alike. Whenever staff members over-step ethical boundaries, intellects remain calm and use the grievance procedure to voice concerns.

- He is always looking for an opportunity to say something positive.

- He is a great communicator.

- He uses prayer, meditation and self-reflection to center himself from prison's daily madness.

- He is a social activist for prisoner's issues.

- He respects women, sees them as more than sexual objects.

- He is overly concerned with issues that move the world. The above points offer further proof why Intellectuals represent the best of those who are or have been incarcerated. As far as reformation is a policy concern Intellectuals are proof positive change is possible and must be a joint venture between prison administrators and prisoners alike. Nothing about this is rocket science. It all boils down to whether or not policy makers and correctional industries care about the product they release back into public domains. In this regard intellectuals offer the best example for implementing educational based policies that deal with the whole prisoner not just punishment for crimes, policies mimicking those capable of transforming deviant thugs into intellectuals.

Context Through Writing

My final goal for this chapter is to show more of the Intellectual's thought process through other writings. In previous chapters I allowed readers to peer into the minds of other characters by way of interviews. I thought a good conclusion for this chapter would be to put forth a number of my personal essays and writings. Nothing more needs to be said at this point. I believe the additional writings stand on their own in their ability to create dialogue and refutation. Enjoy the readings. (These are in the appendix.)

Chapter 12 – The Overseer

"... by the workings of the prison system, society commits every crime against the criminal that the criminal is charged with committing against society..."

-Kate Richards O'Hare in *Prison in 1923*

Rural Wasteland of Isolated Dreams

Rural America was once a vital conduit to America's greatness through agriculture and coal production. Her plains lie barren, victimized by outsourced energy and governmental subsidies that award farmers for not planting crops in an attempt to regulate markets the world over, a critical state of affairs that threatens generational farming. Mom and Pop grocers have taken a backseat to big box stores like Walmart and Target. The same can be said for coal mines. They are increasingly dangerous, dirty, and it has become more expensive to mine out than it is to import. With the inherent hazards of mining, coal miners are going back to school to learn a new trade.

How might Rural America capitalize off uncultivated wastelands? Where there's a will, mankind is adept at creating a way. Outsourcing America's promise (coal and agriculture) doesn't have to be a lose lose proposition. "How about transforming farmland into prisons that we then fill with black and brown corpses?" This is the thing financial dreams are made of. Black and brown bodies are disposable and a nuisance to inner cities. Our brothers from the north will be more than happy to supply us with a constant stream of fresh chattel. When old bodies age out of prison we will fill our empty cells with their sons and grandchildren. We essentially create a never ending economic stream with no overhead using tax dollars to build prisons while paying ourselves in return for babysitting inner city thugs.

"Just think about it. Rural folks will no longer play second fiddle to bogus city municipalities. We will build whole towns off the tragedy of inner city crime that translate into an economic and population boom for rural whites thus giving us the financial means to lobby legislators for harsher criminal penalties and new prison construction. Understand this, city dwellers don't want prisons built in their communities so we are more than happy to convert our farmland into legal plantations, and with the help of Congress and the Judicial process we will render a whole generation of Blacks and Latinos non-existent in America's political, social, and economic experience. The thousands of inanimate bodies we herd into our barbwire plantations will have an even greater affect than Chattel Slavery in that in plain sight we are allowed with the help of Congress and Courts to marginalize minorities by way of mass incarceration. Just think about it: an already fragile community void of strong fearless men disconnected from the tangible aspects of manhood and community building. Devoid of guidance and with diminishing financial opportunities, minority youth will kill one another over illegal crumbs scattered throughout the ghettos."

What does that mean for us? It means the building of more prisons. Each prison can reap 30 to 100 million in tax dollars each year with rural "wastelands" serving a dual purpose:

- The farmer receives money for land usage.

- The building of prisons generates new housing and businesses crop up around prison construction. That's 200 to 300 new correctional jobs available for ex-farmers and coal miners. Not to mention the millions generated off prisoners and their families via overpriced commissary, phone calls, and visit vending machines.

"You see, Agricultural outsourcing and farm subsidies is a win - win proposition for our rural brother, but more than anything we (White America) are allowed to exercise white supremacy through the systematic isolation of black and brown bodies. In the face of a so called Black President and Attorney General this my friend amounts to a legal population control. I wish the law allowed us to vote Mr. Obama in office for two more terms. He's doing such a great job not interfering with our cash cow (prisons). Who says crime doesn't pay? It pays. It just doesn't pay them."

3TGs: The Tyrant, the Thief, and the Truth

Long before Michelle Alexander's book, *The New Jim Crow,* was published, fellow prisoners and I had vigorous discussions around prison economy and prisoners. But what my incarceration has shown me is rural whites working as Correctional Officers thrive in an environment isolated from the rest of the world. They patrol prison grounds like 18 Century plantation owners with their own rules, laws, and social codes. Maybe I'm being a bit too harsh on rural Correctional Officers by calling them plantation owners. How can anyone fault a person for taking advantage of employment? Rural or non-rural I assume any person would be well within their right to seize employment opportunities but what disturbs me is the pompous airs and insensitivity correctional staff show toward the convicted.

A fresh out of college 22 year old frightened female officer quickly takes on the overseer mentality of her male colleagues. I cannot say if her actions are innate or merely a result of group thinking, nonetheless it's demeaning to be ordered around and called all types of vulgar terms and phrases by kids old enough to be my children. From observation it appears 2 out of 20 Co's come to work to do just that, work! Their goal is to return safely home to their family. 18 out of 20 seem to have some type of vendetta against the convicted, thus long after prisoners have been duly sentenced, CO's act as judge, jury and ultimately plantation master.[26] I guess it's true that "power corrupts and absolute power corrupts absolutely." Make no mistake about it, CO's have absolute power over prisoners, backed by the Attorney General's office, The Courts, and Correctional union. Once again, without an independent prison observer separate and apart from Prisons Industrial Complex Prisoner Rights will remain a Human Rights issue.

When I was in free society I imagined like others that prison guards were no more than over paid babysitters for the convicted. As is the case with the inmates, those guards placed in charge over prisoners aren't a monolithic group. Each enters the realm of prison with their individual constructs which show up in their treatment of the bodies which by circumstance have given their lives meaning. As will be illustrated in the paragraphs that follow, I have placed prison guards in three overseer categories: The Tyrant, The Thief, and The Truth; aka Triple T Guards (3TG's)

All 3TGs operate from a position of power and dominance over the men they stand guard over, stemming from an attitude of

---

26 Like prisoners, correctional officers have rules and ethical codes they are obligated to adhere to or face disciplinary measures as stated in Chapter 11. But prison guards violate prison rights daily without consequence due to a faulty grievance procedure. Similarly "the police" in free society have the same problem. CO's protect and hide one another's ethical violations against prisoners. What else is new?

entitlement and a belief that they are superior human beings, although their assumption is as far from reality as the sun is to the moon. For starters it is my premise that anyone who works, participates in and/or draw benefits from an institution that structurally dehumanizes its occupants without offering an avenue for healing is himself functioning from an immoral and reprehensible core. Even when there are a few good apples amongst the officer class, prison's dehumanizing culture causes good officers to conform to prisons defective standards. In any case, even if the so-called 'good guards' win their moral battle, they will ultimately lose bumping up against the ills of the system. For guards and prisoners alike, conformity to ignorance and abuse is the rule if one is to enjoy peace and an above average paycheck with full benefits. The reality is no one who is moral and who possesses a compassionate view of the human experience could enjoy a long and peaceful career as a prison guard. Up first is The Tyrant.

The Tyrant

The state of mind and actions of the Tyrant can be compared to those borne out of a slave plantation where the overseer's sole purpose for existing is to demoralize every slave/prisoner under his charge. The difference is that modern law protects slaves/prisoners from physical abuse. Notwithstanding, physical abuse does occur although it's harder to conceal than the tried and true verbal assault on the slave/prisoner psyche. In plain sight female overseers along with their male colleagues hurl the most vulgar of verbal assaults on slaves/prisoners with greater disdain than feces being flushed down a toilet.

The Tyrant, helped by his or her overseer comrades uses prison rules and codes to assault both minds and bodies of the men occupying prison quarters. The following points offer a look into the activity, behavior and abuses carried out daily by these public officials: activities which escape punishment due to a fraternity that's protected by both courts and correction union alike.

The Tyrant roams prison grounds in the most vindictive and hateful manner. Tyrants often bring personal issues to work where these apparent stresses are exacted on those they oversee. At times it feels like foxes watching over hens by permission of the state. The Tyrant arrives to work with his own public violations which are no different from those of the convicted: violations such as domestic battery, DUI and assault.

They often arrive to work drunk or hung over from the night before.[27] I recall one incident where this particular Tyrant, who was an extreme asshole to everyone it seemed except me, started his work day so intoxicated liquor seeped from his pores. On this particular day while cleaning up my cell I left the door wide open; while making his rounds the overseer stumbled into my cell and hit the floor. Thinking he was stabbed and thus I would be blamed for the stabbing I didn't know whether to run or check his pulse for life. I was so frightened. After verifying he was indeed alive and reeked of alcohol I picked him up and insisted he let me get him some help. He then pleaded for me not to do so because he inevitably would be fired. I complied. The humanity in me saw the human condition and not the social construct of white officer/overseer-black prisoner/slave. I have found that even in our most demoralized states, prisoners tend to be more moral and humane than the individual Tyrants lording over us.

Anyway I proceeded to lay the officer down on my bunk, took his shoes off and made him some black coffee. With little over one hour remaining until we locked up for count I ordered him to rest and ensured him he would be looked after and awakened just before count time. He took me at my word and dozed off.

It should come as no surprise that incident changed the officer in every way imaginable. We became friends and from time to

---

27 When overseers like these enter the prison environment drunk, their colleagues prop them up and deflect attention from them during roll call, after which his fellow overseers, with ranking brass included, place the drunken officer in an inconspicuous post where he can then sleep off his drunkenness.

time he would show his appreciation by bringing me an item or two from the officer's commissary, a relationship that lasted until my transfer from the particular prison. Nonetheless I must say that I experienced a number of petty confrontations with other prisoners for acting humanely to a Tyrant who gave prisoners hell. My fellow prisoners weren't as forgiving. They wanted to see him fired for his treatment of us and that particular incident offered the perfect opportunity for doing so. I felt the sting of their disappointment, but upon seeing the Tyrant's change in behavior toward the broader prison community my prison comrades relaxed their view of my treatment towards the officer.

Tyrants are the biggest work place whores. Every young female cadet entering the prison work environment need not concern herself with the stalking eyes and advances of the incarcerated; their male colleagues give them more attention than they can handle. It's not uncommon for new female guards to sleep with several officers or staff members before learning how to carry her own against prison politics. Lieutenants, majors and other figures like wardens use their authority to procure sexual favors from fragile, docile and financially strapped female guards. Work place harassment is common- place and visible for all prisoners to see. Over the years several female officers have confided in me about their treatment and the pressure to perform sexual favors in exchange for a favorable post or a shift distant from the male prison population.

The Tyrants and overseers in general sleep around with one another's girlfriends, wives and ex-wives. They swap out spouses and mates like dirty underwear for clean ones. Overseers have been observed coming to blows on prison ground over their extracurricular activity.

Tyrants make an already degraded prisoner's life even more degrading by mistreatment. It's as if these types wake up saying, "I owe it to the American public to make prisoners stay miserable without getting myself caught up for an ethic violation." Here is an additional list of The Tyrant's unethical behavior.

1. They use inappropriate language to describe and/or address prisoners. The rules say prisoners are to be addressed by their surnames or prison ID numbers, but unethical officers use terms like convict, faggot, punk, snitch, dick heads, bitches, thugs, gang bangers, and on rare occasions when they are out of ear shot and enjoying what's perceived as a casual conversation with fellow overseers the term "Nigger" slips from their lips. [28]

2. They write tickets for the slimmest infraction without any warning simply because they have the power to do so. They even lie or exaggerate about the severity of the offense.

3. During a routine shake down of prisoner's cells they mishandle prisoners' personal property. Anything they are justified taking they do. Once the Tyrant is done, the cell looks as if a tornado hit it. It could take upwards to one hour to put the cell back in order. This is his way of keeping the slaves off balance and cognizant of his inferior status.

---

28 I witnessed this behavior on several occasions. One time while returning back to my housing after attending the prison library, deep in their conversation and unaware of my presence one overseer dropped three n-bombs. You should have seen their faces when they noticed me standing there. Being the sarcastic individual I am, I stated "so this is how modern slave masters act when no one is watching, huh?" To my statement the overseers replied "Mr. Harvey we weren't referring to prisoners who conduct themselves as men like you, we were talking about those young gangbanger types." I replied. "Well, in that case you were also talking about me, given the man you see in front of you was once one of those gangbanger types you refer to as niggers, before enlightenment reached my soul. It's good to know how y'all (white folks) still think and how little things have changed." I then removed myself from their presence. I felt that if I remained engaged in conversation with them it would reduce the sting of my response. Once I left, I could see them grappling with what had just occurred.

4. During lock-downs prison guards pass out food trays. Prisoners have been heard saying spit was in their food.[29]

5. Tyrants never miss an opportunity to remind prisoners of their permanent underclass status, merely asking a logical question can incur the Tyrant's wrath. His condescending air is so sickening and disrespectful that even when a prisoner is within his right to inquire about this or that he foregoes posing a question to avoid confrontation.

6. Tyrants read prisoners' mail and magazines for kicks. Prisoners often-time receive their magazines and newspapers late in the evening after the C/O is done reading them.

7. During visits the Tyrant flirts with prisoner's girlfriends, wives and family members. They are also known for informing prisoner's spouse and girlfriends about other female visitors. Many relationships have been destroyed in this way.

There is a lot more I could say about this individual but it would be merely overkill. I believe my audience is wise enough to see this characters' foulness without me enhancing his filth. Let's move on to the Thief.

The Thief

The word Thief is often associated with the action and behavior of petty criminals. In this case I use the term to describe Correctional Overseers who knowingly defraud the public of an 8 hour work day. I admit that 17 years ago it didn't much matter how my tax dollars were being spent. I never gave it much

---

29 Lock-downs are the single most dehumanizing moment, where prisoners are made to feel like a dog/pig being fed slop through a rectangle slit in the door. Each night especially during lock-downs, I have to perform some form of metaphysical projection to detox my mind of foul prison stimuli. You must experience it in order to understand what I'm saying.

thought because I was preoccupied with surviving life. Time has a way of maturing us all. The things we overlooked in our immaturity come full circle when we are adults in our thinking.

Observing this Overseer/Slave dynamic has opened my eyes to a number of socio-political occurrences I never gave much thought to until the Prison Complex ensnared me. Consequently I now see it as my duty to expose these Correctional Crooks (we also call them CC's) to the public.

Like many of the characters I have mentioned throughout this process The Thief has several layers as well. I will list each by name along with their job description using an outline format, after which I will cite their pros and cons.

The Correctional Officer/Primary Overseer

Primary Overseer's Roles

- To protect the public from law breakers through isolation.

- To enforce institutional rules which include writing or not writing disciplinary tickets.

- To protect the convicted from being harmed by other convicted/prisoners (which requires CO's to be vigilant.)

- To provide prisoners with lawful necessities such as soap, detergent, toilet tissue, request slips, prison uniforms, cleaning materials (some prisons don't hand out cleaning materials as crazy as that sounds), mail distribution and collection, directions and housing unit supervision.

- Supervise recreation movement.

- Supervise all porter activity and cell movement.

Pros An effective Overseer can provide a ray of hope to the prisoner time-space conundrum in that the inmate is viewed and treated humanely. His apparent overseer status doesn't influence his treatment of those he is given charge over. He's not vindictive. He leaves his worldly issues at the front gate. His demeanor is poised and stress free. He elicits peace and respect from staff and convicts alike. His work place ethics are unmatched.

Cons He is the epitome of stress and gloom. He brings his political, social, and personal issues with him to roll call. He sees all prisoners as despicable scum worthy of ill treatment and himself as the one to exact it. His overseer status uniquely positions him as judge, jury, and executioner. His work place ethics are foul. He uses his position to demean and verbally abuse prisoners in his care. His presence alone fosters a stressful and unsafe prison environment.

Counselors

Counselors' Roles: Serve prisoners' needs

- ○ Provide Information

    - Orientation manual

    - Hand out a number of inmate forms, request slips, money vouchers, grievances, visiting list, phone number add-on list etc.

- ○ Provide Prisoner Services

    - Handle MSR and parole issues.

    - Deal with and address first level grievance issues.

    - Handle transfer request.

    - Link prisoner attorney/court calls.

    - Promote prison programs (GED, vocational school, college, substance abuse etc.

    - Handle good time and loss time issues.

    - Funeral furloughs.

    - Help prisoners handle outside family issues.

Pros A good counselor is to the prisoner as a rudder is to a ship; their value is unmatched by any other prison staffer.

Cons A bad Counselor mentally and emotionally adds dead years to a prison bid. Without the assistant of a good counselor the prisoner is held in correctional limbo from the time he enters prison until his eventual release.

Food Service Supervisor

- Supervise feeding of prison population

- Follow Springfield Dietary Master Sheet.

- Set dietary work schedule for all three shifts.

- Supervise meal preparation

- Supervise prep line and serving of meals

- Issue Special Diets

    ◦ Religious based diets (Kosher, Halal, Vegan etc.)

    ◦ Low-calorie/high calorie meals

    ◦ Low sodium meals

- Supervise cleaning of dietary.

Pros A good food supervisor makes sure food is prepared properly and that portion size is satisfactory. They aren't overbearing and will allow workers the enjoyment of extra helpings.

Cons A bad food supervisor is stressful to work for. They stand over prisoners working the food serving line like a plantation overseer standing over cotton pickers atop a horse. Portion sizes are monitored. When the time arrives for workers to eat, their portion sizes are monitored as well, even when hundreds of pounds of food will be discarded in dumpsters. Waste, waste, waste!

The individual outlined above aren't the only thieves working corrections, they're just the most obvious. There are also teachers, brown and tan shirts (maintenance/engineering types), and Wardens. But due to overseer/slave proximity and/or frequency of interaction, I felt it unnecessary to provide an outline for these latter three.

As far as the Cons are concerned it is representative of correctional norms. Officers and food service supervisors rely on prisoners to do the bulk of their work. These two individuals receive tax dollars for doing no more than watching over the convicted. They (the convicted) are the anchors attached to this correctional ship.

As for counselors the majority are the laziest of all correctional employees in my opinion. Like I mentioned in the pros a good counselor makes serving time more bearable. The social dynamic between counselor and prisoner is different from all other prison staff in that they are the closest link a prisoner has to freedom, therefore the counselor's activity or inactivity stands out more than all other staff persons.

The Truth

If prison reform is to ever become a purposeful reality it starts and ends with the correctional officer especially because they are the primary overseers. In this case I use the phrase The Truth to represent those officers who conduct themselves ethically in every area of prisoner/prison relations. The Truth types are principled individuals. Their anti-establishment mentality allows them to interact with prisoners in a manner that promotes healing to the inmate's concept of self.

Prison work for The Truth is more or less a stepping stone until he or she finishes college or until more meaningful employment opens up. I have had the privilege to discuss issues of life and happiness with a number of these overseer types. Unlike their peers or shall I say colleagues they take no pleasure in being subjugator in chief. The Truth finds common ground with prison

Intellectuals more so than they do with fellow officers. Conversing with prison Intellectual's is the highlight of his day given that prison Intellectual's challenge his humanity and unintentional contribution to deliberate oppression. With all things being equal. I have found The Truth needs the Intellectual just as much as the Intellectual needs the truth. However, prison politics and fraternization policies dampen the natural connection that arises from overseer/slave interaction where classism and punishment out-weigh human social occurrences in order to preserve the structural front of prisons. The Truth is out of place morally. His social conscience prevents him from being an effective Lord over society's defected souls. The moral of this story is, officers such as The Truth are the idea conduit for prison reform, that is, if prison reform is ever to be given serious consideration. It remains to be seen.

Chapter 13- Institutionalized Slaves (IS)

"It's all about me, nothing else matters or makes sense."
-The IS

Greasy, Slithery, Slimy, Sleaze ball! These are attributes of the IS also known as the proverbial "Prison Snitch." His character make up is similar to that of the infamous 18th century "House Nigger." No prisoner is safe from the IS when he detects an opportunity to procure a prison favor or two. They are known to snitch on Overseers, even those they curry favors and perks from. I chose chapter 13 to discuss The IS because like the 13th floor of a traditional office building it's forbidden, The IS shouldn't exist but he does.

What I'm about to say next may appear a bit out of place but given the fact that Illinois prisons are no longer controlled by the various gang factions, security wise, the IS is nearly as important as the warden himself. You might say "how is that so?" Running a successful prison requires knowing the comings and goings of every dangerous individual under the warden's care, therefore eyes and ears must be placed throughout the compound. The safety and security of 2500 or more convicts depend on the service of the IS. Without the information provided by this character, prison plantations would be too dangerous for overseers and prisoner/slaves alike, which by effect would render the warden's position moot for his inability to identify and then isolate prisoners/slaves deemed a security threat.

Generally speaking, prisoners run prison's day to day operation, and like slavery; without prisoners themselves participating in their own imprisonment prisons would be expensive and virtually impossible to operate. In Chapter 9 I provided a list of jobs held by certain prison hustlers but to lend context to my overseer/slave analogy here's a complete list of all available plantation assignments and duties held by prisoners:

1. Porters- Clean prison cell house (including showers). They move prisoners from cell house to cell house. Help pack prisoners personal property after being placed in segregation; during prison lock-downs they pass out food trays alongside overseers; pick up food trays and trash.

2. Cell House Hub Porter- Responsible for cleaning overseer work area. Help check new prisoners into their cells (Think about how that sounds "Help check new prisoners in their cells.)

3. Cell House Laundry Worker- Wash all prisoners' clothes and then pass them back to prisoners.

4. Industrial Laundry and Cleaner Worker – Wash all institutional and hazardous Health Care Unit linen; clean/press/sew overseers uniforms.

5. Maintenance Workers- Keep prison's electrical, plumbing and structural apparatus in top shape for 10 cents a day while being supervised by maintenance overseers who themselves are paid 30 and 40 dollars an hour. Of all prison skilled positions this kind is the most unjust in overall economic devaluation for applied skills.

6. Officer Commissary- Clean commissary area, stock shelves and serve commissary items (coffee, donuts, pizza, etc.) to overseers before work and during lunch breaks.

7. Visiting Room Porter- Keep visiting area clean

8. Clerks- Handle all clerical work for counselors, teachers, maintenance dept. and some administrative office activities.

9. Inside Grounds- Care for prison landscape (grass, flower gardens), garbage and snow removal.

10. Outside Grounds- Care for the front of the prison, garbage and snow removal.

11. Officer Kitchen Workers- Prepare and serve overseers meals; clean kitchen, bus tables, and wash dishes.

12. Institutional Kitchen Cooks- Prep and cook all prison meals.

13. Kitchen Worker- Set-up dinner serving stations, serve meals on standard trays, clean serving lines, bus tables, sweep and mop floors, dishwasher.

14. Prison Commissary Worker- Stock shelves, fill prisoners commissary orders, assist commissary overseer with prisoners commissary check-out.

15. LTS (Leisure Time Services) Worker- Clean gym and exercise equipment, repair broken gym equipment, help organize prison sporting events, in charge of prison band (in most Illinois prisons), help organize social events.

16. Teacher Assistant (TA) – Help teach and tutor other prisoners, in most cases TAs are more effective than the teachers themselves. Imagine the money the state would save by allowing prisoners to teach their fellow prisoners.

17. School Building Porter- Clean, sweep, mop, take out trash in every classroom, wax and buff floors, provide assistance to teachers when needed.

18. Law Clerks- Help prisoners with all legal issues

19. Barber- Cut hair for both overseer and slave.

This assignment list should make it clear overseers are just that, overseers. There is no doubt from a purely structural perspective that prison labor maintains prison plantations. It must also be noted that prisoners aren't the irrational, violent and unruly subgroup correctional officials would have the public believe. If that were the case it would be mathematically impossible for 200 overseers to control 3500 violent offenders without locking down the compound to avoid violence and escape attempts, especially given every inch of prison is run by these so-called violent offenders.

With this in mind it becomes extremely important for wardens and internal officers (IA, for Internal Affairs) personnel to plant their minions amongst the slave population. Prison job assignments are strategic tools wardens and IA use to control prisoners and for information gathering purposes. Although I might add not all who hold plantation job assignments are snitches. The majority of prisoners apply for work detail to either get out of the cell or to earn money for purchasing commissary items.

Being cooped up in a box 18 to 24 hours a day can be traumatizing, so prison work assignments offer mental and physical relief from the stresses caused by our coffin like existence. For the IS type being trapped in a box 24 hours a day is unacceptable, thus he would do whatever it takes to avoid his confines even if that means being the plantation's snitch. As a reward for his espionage the IS is allowed unfettered movement by way of the various job assignments. From what I've come to learn about society through correspondence with those on the outside, IS types aren't specific or unique to prison houses. Corporate America bosses and similar institutions have individuals like these spying on and ratting out fellow employees for perks. Unfortunately what makes the IS such a deprecating soul is his willing contribution to his own subjugation by a bunch of isolated, out of touch, and displaced coal miners and farmers.

Before entering prison I often wondered what was it that made men like those work against their own success in this way? After nearly two decades surrounded by these characters I now know they suffer from self-hatred and a level of ignorance worse than that of chattel slaves. My statement is qualified by the fact 18th century house niggers were deprived of their ability to openly think, act or merely just be. That's not the case today where even under harsh prison conditions prisoners are still capable of being their best selves; after all, I'm writing a book about prisoners and their environment. In plain sight of their overseers, prisoners/slaves, if they so choose to could plot the demise of every prison plantation in America through acquiring knowledge, moral development, and a refusal to provide free labor which on its own merit has the potential to shut down prison complexes. But, when 20th Century plantation dwellers no longer care about their God, Ancestry or the Names they are referred by (inmates, convicts, niggers, pimps, thugs, etc.) it makes it easier for the IS to sell out for plantation perks rather than align himself with fellow prisoners/slaves. In a strange sense I guess the IS's actions are expected given the intelligent design of modern day PICS (Prison Industrial Complex System) that has successfully suppressed any and all intellectual advancement of its inmates.

Victimized 3 or 4 times by the IS myself I have no problem saying that I despise these individuals.[30] Although I understand the psycho-social dynamics surrounding overseer-slave interaction I nevertheless find it hard to digest how someone as low as the prisoner/slave already is would voluntarily work against his collective self. Make no mistake about it, whether he believes it or not, the IS is a part of prison's collective body and experience.

It has not been a joy for me to pen details about this individual but in the grand scheme of PICS, the IS is critical to prison's subjugation of its inmate population and for that, reluctantly, I close this chapter with 3 examples of the IS's cunning plantation activity:

---

30 Prison officials fear any prisoner who has the audacity to defy prison's operant conditioning for higher pursuits, especially when said pursuit seeks political, social, and/or economic gain while in custody. Actions such as these are deemed as participating in unauthorized organizational or security threat group (STG) activity-punishable by segregation and loss of good time credit. Any prisoner who prepares for his future release by writing books, saving money, or securing his intellectual property through the various legal processes (copyright, trade mark, patents) is punished by his host prison for doing so. It is men like these whom the IS character is asked to keep an eye out for by prison administrators.

1. The IS is no stranger to adversity. He comes in and out of prison houses like a skilled stock car driver, maneuvers curves at 100 miles per hour. Knowing the lay of the land he seeks out IA to re-establish his snitching contract. In the IA office he is given the 3W's: Who to watch, When to watch, and What to watch for.

2. Making good on his snitching contract The IS who is often a gang member himself uses his gang affiliation and institutionalized knowledge to hunt down plantation secrets which he then passes on to IA figures. IA then uses the information to isolate and punish any prisoner/slave the IS has identified as a plantation rule violator.[31] The IS is prone to lying and making up false incidents against prisoners he doesn't like or those not affiliated with the gang he runs with. This is where The IS power is more pronounced because plantation authorities use the snitches words against the prisoner in question without being afforded due process. The IS's lying tongue is the law.

3. The IS uses his plantation assignment to gain close proximity to all prison classes. He then befriends individuals deemed to be high profile in nature (gang leaders, radicals, intellectual types, and prison hustlers who run gambling operations and the likes.)

What dealing with the IS has shown me is that modern prisoners are intellectually inadequate, immoral, and unsophisticated, thus unable to wage a collective stance against prison's inherit sickness. In order for prison to exist deficient characters must be given free reign to do the overseer's bidding, nonetheless prisoner/slaves are ultimately responsible for their own mental and social condition while serving time. Unfortunately the proverbial snitch isn't going

---

31 Punishment often comes in the form of segregation, loss of good time credit, and relocation to a different prison with higher security restriction and a thousand miles from family members. Depending on security severity i.e. drug and/or knife possession, snitch victims can be given a new charge and arraigned in court.

anywhere, he is as much a part of the prison structure as barbwire is to fencing.

Appendices

Appendix -2

Disloyal Chattel

The Correspondence of Marcus and Jonathan

by

Tyrone F Muhammad

December 2010

Narrator: The student athlete Marcus sits at a picnic table outside the University of the American Dream (UAD) near the south-end parking lot. While waiting for his next class to begin, Marcus decides to catch up on his correspondence with his high school friend Jonathan who is serving six years in prison for selling drugs. When they were both in high school, Marcus was the back-up running back to Jonathan who was at the time considered the nation's top running back.

Marcus: I received your last letter Jonathan, I'm happy to hear you are still taking college courses in the joint. I'm sorry to hear about the insensitivity of public lobbying to shut down college in prison programs throughout America. What harm is it causing society to teach prisoners how to fish for their own food instead of panhandling someone else for fish? It makes absolutely no sense to me.

The way I see it, either society will become excited and inspired by the ex-cons' ability to catch their own fish, or they can continue to put up with ex-cons taking their hard caught meal. Either way society will have to spend money protecting their fish from those who don't have any. I really hope a legislator come along who sees the value in reforming prisons as a logical undertaking. I guess no matter where you're at, the politics of man finds permeation, even in prison.

Jonathan, I must tell you the truth, with each passing day I grow more dissatisfied by the choice I made to attend college on scholarship. My being here is starting to feel so unethical. The coach's control our lives; it's tantamount to a jockey controlling the reins of a thoroughbred racing horse. I feel like a big idiot.

Just the other day I attempted to express my feelings about college to Coach Pataki, and he ripped me a new ass-hole. His words were so demeaning I felt lower than a peasant, worse than a slave. His words to me were, "You listen to me Marcus, I have a problem with the way you have treated this college generosity. How dare you talk about leaving school after we have invested our time and dollars developing your talent. We have a great investment in your body. You are the most

Appendix -4

ungrateful student athlete I've ever had the opportunity to work with. When I found you in the slums of your ghetto reality you had nothing. You lived in the projects with your Momma and your thuggish ways were bound to land you in prison where they warehouse all the other thugs."

"Remember all the strings we pulled to make you academically eligible to attend our prestigious learning institution? What about the time you arrived on campus lost from all social activities and we introduced you to every prominent person on campus and even to our daughters? We exalted you like no other thug, and when you needed financial assistance we slid you a few extra dollars under the table."

"Marcus, to be perfectly honest you haven't earned the right to complain about anything. We tell you when to practice, what to eat, how to dress, and what time to go to bed. So what we make millions off your talent? – we took you out of those slums and instilled in your our doctrine. So ask yourself where would you be without the charity of a sports scholarship?"

"Just as I figured! You wouldn't be receiving an education from the University of the American Dream; instead your scholarship would come from the University of Prison. How dare you even think about leaving school after we invested time and money developing your talent. I hope you understand what you're doing. Now get out of my office."

Marcus: You see what I mean about being treated like a thoroughbred?

Narrator: Jonathan had so much talent that NFL Scouts attended his high school games. During football practices Jonathan would teach Marcus certain techniques to maximize his ability as a running back. Jonathan was also known as one of the biggest drug dealers in his community. Before prison caught up with him, he made certain his buddy Marcus wore the latest gear and had money in his pocket to sustain himself. Now with Jonathan no longer around to provide financially,

Marcus has grown overly concerned with the monetary end of his college experience. Marcus' views of being used by UAD are causing him to lose sight of his primary purpose for accepting his scholarship in the first place.

Marcus: Often when I write you I sit at my favorite picnic table near the south parking lot. I watch 18 year old kids pass me by in $50,000 whips. What have they done to deserve such luxuries? Who do they know? I bet they never had to fight or struggle for anything in their life. They wouldn't know what hard times look like if it smacked them in the face. And to think these – our future leaders – are expected to understand the plight of the poor?

I remember asking Marty, one of the more well-off students in my sociology class, what he intended on doing with his education. He told me "I don't intend to do anything with it. I'm in college because it's what my parents wanted." You see most of these kids are in school for the wrong reason. They drive by with their high society airs without a care in the world with the exception of those whom I sign autographs' for, everyone else seems so snobbish. I wonder if they understand it is talent like mine which gives this place its prestige? If it weren't for the physical abilities of student athletes like me who would pay for all those $100,000 plus salaries of college professors? Last year the UAD made $5 million off our efforts on the field and that's just off stadium ticket sales. The figure doesn't include advertisement and memorabilia sales. How much of that money do student athletes receive? Where's my $50,000 BMW for performing well on the field?

Can you believe I was given a three game suspension for accepting a $100 jersey as a gift? I thought this was the craziest thing in the world because my school sells over five hundred of my jerseys each week for which I'm not permitted to receive any monetary compensation. I'm in trouble for receiving my own jersey as a gift. This is unbelievable! I feel so used up, my college education for four years is only worth $160,000. I'm no mathematician. In fact, don't even like math, but it doesn't take a college degree to compute the financial imbalance of the university against its student athletes. I'm given a food and expense stipend of $250.00 a month. When you were home I didn't have the financial worries I'm now faced with. Here other students don't even have to work since their parents are well off, their living expenses and personal wants are covered. They only have to focus on getting good grades through study. Tell me, brother, if all the drama I'm going through is worth receiving a college scholarship? The pressure I'm under to maintain a "C" average is stressing me out. Receiving an education shouldn't be such a headache, especially when every citizen should be afforded an education regardless of how many plays he or she makes on the field. How is this fair Jonathan? Why is it permissible for educational institutions to exploit the physical abilities of its citizens just to receive something due to them as citizens.

Narrator: A few admirers drive up in a convertible blowing their horn to get the attention of their favorite student athlete. Marcus stops writing, put his pen down, flashes a phony smile and waves back to his adoring fans. Marcus immediately goes back to writing.

Marcus: I don't really want to be here. I recognize I'm out of my element. Plus I'm not feeling the teaching style of UAD professors, this 'banking style' of teaching practiced by so many professors doesn't allow students to develop their individualism. Don't get me wrong, forcing students to learn certain knowledge is a necessary part of development, but not all knowledge is usable knowledge.

Narrator: Five minutes later Marcus' adoring fans make it over to his table for autographs. He signs them and turns his attention back to writing to Jonathan.

Marcus: For instance, I'm forced to take classes I care absolutely nothing about, just to receive a piece of paper. I thought receiving an education was about developing the inherent uniqueness of each student. Tell, what does learning about a bunch of white colonizers in an era of manifest destiny, slave labor, and civil war, going to do to help me put food on my family's table?

To be honest, learning about former slave owners only increases my anxiety about existing in a society which has given my ancestors so little while taking so much. I tell you, having knowledge of America's historical illnesses has affected my ability to be fully and truly socialized. Some of these very institutions of learning we run up and down the field for were founded by slave owners themselves. How ironic is that? Better yet, oxymoronic is that? Can you say 'moral and intellectual hypocrisy?'

Narrator: Marcus' Coach sold him on the idea that playing football for the University of the American Dream was the greatest opportunity he had to get his mother and sisters out of those notorious Chicago Projects. With his best friend being incarcerated, Marcus doesn't trust anyone else to share his feelings with. So he expresses his emotions through his correspondence with Jonathan to give him a picture of what he's experiencing on campus.

Marcus: Man, Jonathan, these hidden emotions have taken me so far off course of my original thought. Please forgive my ranting. This imbalance of University – Athlete relationship is eating me so deep in my soul, so deep it's affecting my play on the field. Can you believe I was suspended 3 games for accepting a $100 jersey as a gift? I hope my suspension doesn't frighten scouts away. You would think my 1300 yards would be enough to convince any NFL scout or team to look past my youthful indiscretion of accepting a gift.

Besides I didn't know it was illegal to receive a present; what harm did I cause? It wasn't like anyone gave me $10,000 to fumble the football. The scrutiny we are under, the restrictions place on us 18-20 year olds is unbearable. Just because I'm a student athlete why should I be exempt from making the same mistakes other 18 year olds make? Playing organized sports is no longer fun for me. I feel less than human. It appears as though student athletes have become nothing but objects placed on display to attract corporate dollars. So when we as student athletes make a mistake it's viewed as the college property making a public relations blunder against the purity of the school.

The things we go through to receive an education are unfair, the only other youth population exploited to receive an education as students athletes are the soldiers in the various US Armed Forces. The tragedy for this group is the fact some soldiers will never return home to benefit from signing up to protect our so-called freedoms. When their flag draped coffins return from war zones what is the value then of a GI Bill they will never use? How sad a reality is that, Jonathan?

Lastly, I don't have the desire to be here but by some strange twist of fate I've been given an opportunity that's more fitting to serve your needs than mine. You and I both know you are a better athlete than I could ever imagine being. Without any effort you would out-perform everyone on any university football field I've played on. This is the type of environment you would absolutely thrive in. In comparison for the layout of our neighborhood the campus aesthetics is synonymous to heaven on earth. The landscape is absolutely magnificent.

I've taken up enough of your time with all my complaining so I will end my word for now. Take care and be safe in there. Write back soon I'll put some money on your books this week. Your Brother and friend, Marcus.

Narrator: Jonathan relaxes in the comfort of his tight cell, drinking a cup of green tea when the C/O enters the cell, handing him 3 pieces of mail. Two letters are from his high school sweetheart Keisha and the third one from his best friend Marcus. He made it a point to always read Marcus' letter first because his letters gave him a glimpse into the university life that escaped him due to prison. After reading Marcus' letter and thereby reflecting on the contents, Jonathan put everything he was working on from his prison college class on hold, to give his friend's letter the needed attention.

Jonathan's response to Marcus:

Jonathan: I pray my letter finds you feeling much better than the spirit I received from your last correspondence. Marcus, I will try not to take too much of your time since you're in final exam season, nevertheless, what you are experiencing demands my full attention if you're to enjoy continual success. My goal today is to bring your mind back into focus before you become completely blinded by the irrationality of your emotions.

I read your letter three times, to grasp your thought process, and from what I've gathered your words fail to gauge the moral decadence of the roach infested hood we both come from. Have you forgotten about that reality? Surely, you've recognized while sleeping in the comfort of your dormitory that there were no sounds of gun shots and drugs being sold on every corner?

You complain about your $250 a month food stipend, but do you recall those days when food was scarce in both our households and we still managed to survive? What about those days we made sandwiches and we were happy to have all the ingredients on hand because Lord knows there were plenty of times we had peanut butter with no jam or vice versa. But did that stop us from enjoying what little we had? No it didn't! In fact, those hard times only inspired us to dream about creating a better life for ourselves and our family. Have you forgotten about the promise we made to ourselves to win in this game of life by any means necessary, even on the football field? Marcus, you know that's the reason why I started selling drugs in the first place – so we could eat whatever we wanted to.

Right now, Marcus, it is necessary that you remain steadfast and focused on the bigger picture. You stated in your letter that you have been reading about the historical nature of our country, then you are well informed as to Adam Smith's capitalistic theory? Make no mistake about it, you and I are the product of a nation rooted in capitalism. If that wasn't the case, why do we sell drugs in our communities to our own people: I'll tell you why! Because of a thing called supply and demand. If

Appendix -10

there wasn't a market for the sales and distribution of drugs, we could do no business; this is the American way. You see Adam Smith's market principles don't just apply for the things society deems legal, but also those things society deems illegal, as long as there's a demand or a market for the product.

The problem arises when the so-called disadvantaged segments capitalize on the same system of exploitation without cutting the founders of exploitation in on the profits via taxes, fines, under-the-table handouts, etc.

So there you have it. Whether the demand is for prisons, military bases or universities, there's an inherent need for bodies to fill those spaces. The difference lies in what each party is willing to give up in order to achieve their personal objective. The first colonizers chose to give up their soul to become great by decimating two classes of human being: Native Americans, and dark skinned people from the diaspora of Africa. The natives and Africans are still suffering from those ills. The personal objective I chose was to no longer live a life of want and need. As we both know, that was a short-term objective with long-term consequences, which in the end has proved to be an unwise choice. Although you, my family, and others benefited from my illegal actions, my actions have isolated me from those I was selling drugs to support or so I thought. Who's supporting you all now that I'm no longer around? Yes, you're right, I was a top athlete but I wasn't any good in school or in taking orders from others. You know my radical way of viewing things would never allow some coach who's not my father to yell, scream and spit in my face. No sir, I would have been in prison for punching the coach in the mouth. Trust me, college at that time in my life wasn't for me. I was too immature for the process of growth that an environment like college is innately intent on producing. You, on the other hand, might not be the athlete I was, but your ability to grasp logical concepts and your love for literature and art places you at the forefront of academia. Unlike me, even if you don't make it to the NFL, you'll do fine in the bigger societal scheme of things.

Just look at how you critically broke down the monetary injustice of the university against its student athletes. You will do just fine.

As you know, it took my coming to prison and getting with a higher learning program called Education Justice project (EJP) to understand the brain should be used for more than bagging up cocaine packs and chasing promiscuous girls. What am I saying to you, Brother? I'm saying my critical thinking capacity came about as a result of coming to prison, where in your case you were thinking critically before you went to college. That's why you never sold drugs. You thought it was illogical to risk life in prison pursuing ill-gotten gains. Your assessment obviously rang true; my current predicament is a testament to your insight.

Now you write me complaining about the monetary disadvantages of your college scholarship vs. the university's profiting off student athletes. My question is when did you become so concerned about material wealth? Money has never been your reason for doing anything. Tell me then, how does watching rich white kids cruise around campus in $50,000 whips all of a sudden make you dissatisfied? Marcus, you are a brilliant thinker, you already understand the social dynamics that allow those kids to enjoy the pleasures of life. Besides, how can you fault those 17-18 year olds for having rich parents stupid enough to buy them $50,000 cars? They don't have to do anything to earn such a gift. The very nature of their birth affords them the right to enjoy the fullness of the American Dream. It's not those kids' fault they are white and as a consequence thereof rich. Your focus should be on how you will use your university experience to maximize your chances of being able to buy your child a $50,000 car in the future if you so choose. Keep your focus on making it out of there and not getting shot by campus police for being a black man on a college campus. Furthermore, who told you attending college would be a cake walk? Marcus, until you achieve your goal to get your mother and sister out of those Chicago projects, you must act as if you're being forced to walk a pirate's plank. College for you has to be a critical experience, not a material pity party. You can't afford to have fun and material abundance until you prove your value and ultimately your worth to society. In your case, prove your worth on the football field for NFL Scouts.

My Brother, I know things are hard but you must remain steadfast and succeed for all of us in the Hood. Your success is our success. Everyone is rooting for you, even the homies in prison. Whenever we see you running up and down the field on ESPN we are all inspired. Look man, you know my story. You know my crime. If I could do things differently, I would be on campus with you. I would rather deal with the exploitative nature of the university prison than the Prison Industrial Complex I'm subjected to. So, Brother, I don't want to hear any more complaining because you have the will to endure. And remember, you made it out of the hood and have a whole class of men counting on you to succeed, especially me.

Marcus, the following words express how it feels living in a box with nowhere to turn except to my imagination for inspiration. Read these words and gain insight. My condition should be all the encouragement you need to succeed.

Looking beyond the window of my shell I explore the limits of my mind confined in a cell:

420 Blocks[32]

Locked in a Box

Guards on the Clock

Soap in a Sock[33]

Sleeping on a Cot

---

32 420 is the number of 14" x 8" blocks I count in my cell when I'm bored and can't sleep.

33 Soap in a sock is the oldest and most accessible prison weapon available

Tears in Hock

Frozen by the decree of time,

Folded or molded by the moisture of the mind:

Isolate Stock

Living out of a Box[34]

Trapped with a Flock

That plots around the Clock

Abandoned dreams of a boy born to be King

what joy is there to bring

What songs left to sing?

Through you I float my hopes;

With your success the 'hood' receives its rope.

Take care, my friend. I'll write again in a few days.

Sincerely, Jonathan

Narrator: after reading Jonathan's letter three times at his favorite picnic table, student athlete Marcus reflects on his family's condition and his purpose for accepting his university scholarship. The follow words reflect Marcus' thinking out loud, having read Jonathan's letter.

Marcus: Whoa! What's wrong with me? How did I allow myself to become so distracted? I must not lose focus of why I attended college. Jonathan is right. There are absolutely too many people depending on me. It is imperative I relax my views in order to accomplish my goal. The injustice taking place on college campuses are issues I can take up as a cause when I make it to the NFL. Stay focused, Marcus, you have to get your mother and sisters out of that horrific public housing. Poverty

---

34 Living out of a box simply means the cell is box like; property is stored in a box, and food we eat comes out of boxes.

Appendix -14

has been the religion of my family for generations. My talent got me here; it will take a rational mind to keep me here.

Narrator: During game day, student athletes are made aware of the section where NFL scouts are seated. The student athletes try to impress upon NFL scouts their individual talents.

Marcus: Tomorrow is my first game back after being suspended. Man it feels like forever. I don't know if I could live without football. I will never do anything stupid to keep me off this field again. I own the football field. The only time I'm at peace is when I'm receiving and dishing out punishment within that one hundred yard space. Tomorrow I will get my numbers on that field whether I win or lose. These scouts will be watching and I will leave a lasting impression on them. They will see the fierceness and urgency in every run I make on the field. When the ball is in my hand I now run for my family, and that includes you, Jonathan.

Structural Intent of Prisons

Tyrone F Muhammad

INTRODUCTION

Since modern time man's preoccupation with the State's welfare has compelled rational homo sapiens to institute laws and maxims that are concerned with the ethical behavior of individuals sharing the same open space. It is therefore by virtue of laws and maxims that individual freedoms are preserved, and likewise enforced. Although in contrast, when those very institutions of laws and maxims are unable to regulate individual 'states of characters'[1] proving detrimental to spaces of freedom, then, the participants in society must rise to action by creating institutions (e.g. asylums, reformatories, and prisons) for isolating those persons from the populace and from harming themselves.

Prisons in this case are the structures in question, as they purport to be legislative mechanisms for correcting deviancy. Nevertheless it is my belief prisons in their current formation has outgrown their usefulness and therefore must undergo radical reconstruction in order to live up to their legislative and judicial intent. This paper examines the virtue of prisons and their inability to bring about moral reformation of those being released back into society. As a question of 'deficit and means'[2], prisons as a whole seem to place more credence on the activity of punishment as evidence of quantitative engagement rather than on the qualitative deliverance of person back into domains of freedom.

Where reform is concerned, this paper put forth a four (4) point approach towards achieving that end. Wherefore, the reformation of individual states of character ought to be the goal of penal institutions, since "to do" reform is 'virtuous activity'[3] It is clear prisons have fallen ethically short in this regards. Not only have they become moral infractions on society and its occupants, they are also civil and economical failures as well. Prison officials have consistently released ex offender's back into society without a system for assessing their mental and social capacity to dwell alongside other law abiding citizens. And since prisons aren't going anywhere soon, let's take a look at a few historical accounts of prisons and their sociopolitical underpinnings.

CONFINEMENT, HISTORY and RATIONALE

The inclination to confine human beings for acts of malice and ill contempt is as long as time itself. When viewed from a biblical context the bible is riddled with examples of confinement and punishment as a notion of character 'habituation'[4.]

For example, in the monotheistic story of Prophet Joseph the reader is presented with a number of narratives examining the misapplication of power and punishment. Where Joseph is the subject of confinement, the authorities of his day never took into account his exceptional character. We know as a result of scriptural observation the King's only cause for granting Joseph judicial reprieve was due in part to his God given ability to interpret dreams, and therefore it was a question of political means and utility not justice. Again, Joseph's moral ideation or character was never given consideration by the King or any other authority until Joseph himself made it the basis for his release. Similar in kind, today's prisons are just as ineffective when it comes to assessing and correcting the character of those it isolate. Structures for punishment have to be more than about penalties for crime.

Penalties for criminal activity can be seen in 7th century BCE Athens where the law giver "Draco" issued death penalties for meager offenses. Like the prevailing views of our current law makers, Draco believed that harsh penalties equated to less criminal activity because it was thought to instill in potential law breakers fear of the consequences of crime. Today's criminological research and high recidivism has proven "Draconian" notions of punishment are equally ineffective as that of modern day Retributionists' formulation of "just deserts" for bad acts also known as "truth and sentencing laws". In fact, excessive sentencing has only caused a prison population boom rather than a decrease in crime.

Similarly in eighteenth and nineteenth century Europe before the institution of a constitution, Monarchs and Noblemen established laws and issued decrees that punished law breakers. The penalties were extremely harsh, even minor infractions warranted capital punishment. (Hudson 1996 p. 19) For some, harsh penalties are enough to turn deviant individuals into law abiding citizen. Although statistics show the majority of ex-prisoners will re-offend without an outside force interrupting their cognitive notions of crime as a means to 'happiness'[5.]

This brings to mind the theoretical assertion of those who advocate 'Restorative Justice' as a means to not only punish offenders but to also restore the offender to useful citizenship before and after their release[6]. As a basis for healing the community, restorative justice engenders the biblical discourse of Jesus in Mathew 25 highlighting the ethical treatment of fellowmen, regardless of their social, economic, and political station in life. It's rational to presume Jesus disapproved of the treatment of prisoners as observed in Matthew 25 Verses 43 & 45:

43 :I was a stranger, and ye took me not in: naked and ye clothed me not: sick, and in "Prison", and ye visited me not.

45 :Then shall he answer them saying, Verily I say unto you, Inasmuch as ye did it not to one of the least of these, ye did it not to me.

Verse 43 mention prisons by name, maybe it's a stretch, but I'm of the opinion Jesus saw prison as dens of denigration that marginalized the prisoner from the broader community. As a question of moral resolve, it is my view that Jesus is urging the believers to righteousness and too be mindful of their duty and how they treated even the least amongst them, prisoner included. It is with this verse more than any other that the public and prison administrators are reminded to be just in matters of treatment and punishment.

In theory, crime prevention through long periods of incapacitation (a term used by the Retributivist for separating bad individuals from society) appears sound until recidivism rates bring into question the efficacy of confinement absent of a viable system for rehabilitation. Incapacitation for the sake of isolation is clearly a retributivist notion. But we know by observing prison overcrowding that incapacitate alone hasn't prevented crime or recidivism. In fact, it can be objectively argued that incapacitation on its own has been actually counterproductive to crime prevention. From a purely ethical perspective prisons have systematically turned in on themselves, where the answers for fixing crime respond in theory similar to the proverbial band aid on a leaky pipe.

A FOUR POINT PROGRAM FOR VIRTUOUS REFORM

This brings me to my core argument, prisons as structures for isolating defected characters has historically acted in a way that is problematic for the state and the prisoner where it consistently brings into question the state's obligation to reform. As an economical question, if prisons were fortune 500 companies they would be bankrupted due to the product (prisoner) liability of the manufacturer (that being prisons). The only way to properly measure prison effectiveness is by gauging recidivism rates. This formulation suggests two critical aspects of confinement that precede my four point program, one being economic; the other being rehabilitative.

I surmise daily routines and monitored regimen (e.g. school, work, and therapy) can and will act on the 'criminal man' in ways that prison sentences void of purposeful activity can't. In this Aristotle would agree, for his words are congruent with my logic, he states: "For the things we have to learn before we can do them, we learn by doing them, e.g. men become builders by building and lyre players by playing the lyre; so too we become just by doing just acts, temperate by doing temperate acts..." (Aristotle p.23) Although Aristotle's quote doesn't reference prison in this instance, it nevertheless follows along the same logical line.

Just as men learn to build and play lyre by building and playing, so to must right conduct and decriminalization be established by a process of habituation. On the same page of the above quote, Aristotle places blame chiefly on state legislators to make its citizens better individuals by forming good habits in them. Notwithstanding, "every art and every inquiry, and similarly every action and choice, is thought to aim at some good; and for this reason the good has rightly been declared to be that at which all things aim" (Aristotle p.3) I contend this quote affixes itself to the prison structure like water to earth. If Aristotle is correct in his assertion, then, prison as a whole "ought" to aim at some good. Its (Prison's) actions and similarly the choices it makes necessarily affects its occupants, and must provide avenues for transformative thought if the activity of correction is to be achieved. The following four point approach grapples with the age old problem of recidivism: by instituting psycho-social mechanisms that prompt rehabilitation over revenge through excessive punishment.

POINT #1: INTERVENTION OF CRIMINAL THOUGHT USING PSYCHO-THERAPY AND LIFE COACHES:

"The exercise of discipline presupposes a mechanism that coerces by means of observation; an apparatus in which the techniques that makes it possible to see induce effects of power and in which, conversely, the means of coercion make those on whom they are applied clearly visible. "(Foucault p. 18)

The formulation behind point #1 brings into view the above quotes by Foucault which see punishment as an apparatus of discipline where properly executed techniques must affect through coercion the body of the inmate. By proximity Foucault believed there could not be coercion without a set of orders (e.g. a law, a program, and a set of regulations) that subject the offender to rigorous observation. (Foucault p. 189, 195)

Notwithstanding, point #1 challenges every offender who enters prison gates to look at their decision for choosing crime as a "means to an end", as well as look into the psycho-social state deemed necessary to perform such permanent activity. On the first day of prison each offender will be assigned a Psychotherapist and Life Coach; also known as Secondary Observer (SO's), for the duration of their sentence. Principle observation in this case is executed by Primary Observer (PO's) (e.g. Wardens, Correctional Officer, and Parole Personal). Each offender will be scheduled for psychotherapy session once every 60 days and once every 120 days to his life coach.

Because prisoners are consistently transferring to other prisons, SO's are required to keep detailed and up dated files. Prisoner files are subjected to review at any time by prison administrators to help gauge the prisoner progress or regress. It is my expectation to develop a manual to be used by every SO or CO to get the greatest effect from psycho-social therapy. This is an ethical task that will prove to deliver grand results.

POINT #2: PROVIDE EDUCATIONAL COMPULSION FOR ALL PRISONERS REGARDLESS OF SENTENCE AND AGE:

"Virtue, then, being of two kinds, intellectual and moral, intellectual virtue in the main owes both its birth and its growth to teaching (for which reason it requires experience and time), while moral virtues comes about as a result of habit... (Aristotle p. 23)

The importance of an informed and educated citizen can no longer be taken for granted. It was told to me "one child drops out of school every 26 second". This is a moral travesty with criminal consequence, given the fact a number of America's dropouts end up in prison. It appears from observation that what doesn't come out in "The Wash" (The Educational System) shows up in "The Rinse" (The Prison System). Unfortunately it is within prison settings that most dropouts study how to become master criminals. Without an external mechanism working on the offenders new found concepts of criminal behaviors, prison then becomes symbolic school for fostering future bad acts that continue to violate the community at large. Therefore the implementation of a viable education policy is critical if meaningful reforms are to be accomplished.

Since most incarcerated men come from broken environments with fractured identities, educational programs must not only build intellect but also shake a prisoner out of his/her cultural comfort zone. This is very important inasmuch as the idea behind drug dealing, gang banging, and overall criminality stems partly from a misapplication of knowledge that rationalizes bad acts as a means to power and thereafter social inclusion. The following three principles offer the best chance for learning:

1. Every offender upon entering prison will be assessed academically and subsequently placed in the appropriate living quarters germane to prisoner's educational needs (ABE. GED, Vocational Training, and College Degree).

2. Educational pursuit must be the basis for rewarding the offender privileges (e.g. T.V., Radio, Hot Pot, etc.)—not prison politics e.g. who you are or who you snitch on).

3. Any offender who has not achieved his GED is not allowed to work prison jobs in place of those who have—since to be out and about the prison cell imply a certain privilege of movement. All jobs must be merit base, not quid pro quo. Every prisoner will be issued state pay based on his academic accomplishment and not merely as a stipend due to him by virtue of his confinement.

Rationale:

It is my belief these principles will necessarily induce the offender to strive for more while serving his sentence. For the offender serving prison time alone is hard enough, but, when the offender has to serve a sentence devoid of T.V.'s, Radio's, and other human comforts it makes doing time even more unbearable. It is my hope these three elements in and of themselves ought to induce offenders towards activities that are meaningful and activities that can be carried over to society. Since most offenders will choose "idleness" over study and intellectual edification, they must be made to feel the effect of choosing badly. It is with this rationale that the implementation of knowledge through learning offers the best chance against recidivism.

POINT #3: WORK OPPORTUNITY THAT FOSTERS GOOD HABITS AND DEVELOPS USEFUL SKILLS IN THE OFFENDER

"To love work is essentially a noble characteristic; and therefore, any life without work as its cornerstone is a life lived ignobly". (Tyrone F. Muhammad)

Work as an activity is that thing developed in youth. As a question of virtue through habituation, it appears from observation that most prisoners lack the necessary skill and work ethic to earn a viable living upon release. It is with this understanding that crime for the ex-offender is more utilitarian and not necessarily one finding pleasure in the activity of debauchery and deviancy.

Point #3 institute elements for habituating offenders to work as an option to crime. Current prison structure allows offenders to sit idle in cells 18 to 24 hours daily without urging work related activities. All prisoners from day one will be assigned:

1. Each offender will be assessed through an interviewing process to determine work history and career aspiration

upon release. Only offenders with sensible projected out dates will be assessed in this manner.

2. Each offender will be required to attend a week long seminar on the benefit of work and a week-long class on economics.

3. Upon completion of the work seminar the counselor will assign each offender a full-time prison job specific to his or her skill-set or future career aspiration as determined by initial interviewing process. The offender pay grade must reflect commissary price inflation as well as offender's skill-set.

4. In an effort to release offender back into society a more responsible, fully functional individual, 5 to 10% of offender's pay will be saved with interest and released to offender upon completion of sentence. The cost benefit of this act is tremendous as it eliminate thousands in prison gate money and transportation cost. On the back end of such an initiative ex-offender is given a sense of pride by being released with money he earned.

Rationale:

Nothing builds confidence in a man more than having a marketable skill or vocation by which financial success is ensured. And since the majority of offenders enter prison deficient in work related activity it is incumbent upon the state to institute corrective measures that challenge and/or foster some sort work habit in those they are given ward over. Although it is true that crime takes on a number of forms, it is nonetheless true that most criminal activity seek financial gain, and therefore, criminality tend to be economic in nature. This is not just from the offender's perspective but judicially and legislatively as well. Finally to develop in the offender work related habits and marketable skills is a moral undertaking, with social ramification that extends beyond the ex-offender into the broader community.

POINT #4: A VIABLE PAROLE PROCESS THAT NOT ONLY REGULATE OFFENDERS' BEHAVIOR, BUT WORK TO BRING HEALING TO THE VICTIMS AND/OR VICTIM FAMILY

"Now the worst man is he who exercises his wickedness both towards himself and towards his friends, and the best man is not he who exercises his virtue towards himself but he who exercises it towards another, for this is a difficult task." (Aristotle p.82) A correctional system deficient in its consideration for the victim well-being acts unethical in matters of reconciliation. Point # 4 brings to bear the prisoner's responsibility to affect healing of the victim by way of legislative initiatives that extends justice beyond mere confinement. Such initiatives include but are not limited to:

1. The payment of fines for acts of violence against another to be assessed upon conviction; based on the severity of the criminal act; and to be carried over after release.

2. To require all offenders to attend a yearly seminar on justice as rectification that highlights the inequities inherent in the committing of crime and its effect on its victims.

3. Once the offender is situated and assigned to work, once a month 10% of the offender's pay will be set aside for expiation and retribution and sent to the victim or victim family.

4. To institute a program that offers an opportunity for healing both victim and victimizer through a process of dialogue that allows the victim to confront the victimizer within a secured environment. Understandably, this requires both victim and victimizer to agree to the confrontation. A program such as this can prove valuable for those demanding closure to move on with life.

5. Along with the inherit parole obligation the offender upon release will be required to perform community service applicable to his or her crime (e.g. Domestic Violence

volunteer, City Morgue volunteer. Troubled Youth counseling etc.).

Rationale:

As someone who has come to love justice and fair play. I am of the view that victims of crime are forgotten and the victimizers for the most part are only required to serve time. Not that serving is easy, but in my opinion it fails to help offenders to consider the victims' psycho-social health as well as to identify with the offenders own issues of deviancy.

In conclusion, the ideals behind this paper, I must admit are quite ambitious, nevertheless they are ideas I believe offer a viable option and/or addition to the current system being applied to correct men of ill repute. As a society ruled by ethics and laws we can no longer sit back leaving things as they are without putting forth meaningful resolutions that challenge every prisoner to excellence regardless of the nature of the offense. Although I was unable to answer every question and address every concern in this discourse, nonetheless, I do believe the contents offer plenty to begin a fruitful conversation about the ethics in prison reform.

BIBLIOGRAPHY:

1. Aristotle. The Nicomachean Ethics, Oxford University Press. 2009.

2. Bazemore, G. and M. Schiff. "What and Why Now: Understanding Restorative Justice." Cincinnati, OH. Anderson. 2001.

3. Foucault, M. Discipline and Punishment—The Birth of Prison. Vintage Books. 1979.

4. Hudson, B. Understanding Justice: An Introduction to Ideas, Perspectives and Controversies in Modern Penal Theory. Buckingham, England: Open University Press. 1996.

5. Rabinow, P. The Foucault Reader. Pantheon Books. New York. 1984

Endnotes

1. States of character is those things of virtue Aristotle say deals with the degree of good or bad conduct as well as how we conduct ourselves when affected by emotions and passion, p.28

2. A play on Aristotle's formulation of defect, excess, and means— where in this case my use of deficit take on two meaning, one which question the ineffective use of prison; the other which question the character deficit of prisoners being released back into society unreformed, and in a worst character state then when they first entered.

3. Aristotle believed all activity "ought" to aim at some good, in this case prisons as structures "ought" to be ethical in the reformation process of men entering her gates, and therefore such activity is deemed an excellent virtue, p.30

4. In this case habituation is concerned with character development using prison as a mechanism for producing good habits in bad men. According to Aristotle it is difficult to expect men who haven't been brought up under right law to live or act in ways that are virtuous without being habituated in a way which foster's it. p. 199-200

5. Happiness for Aristotle is what all things aim towards (even animals). It's also true then that criminal activity, although an immoral activity, seeks a means to an end and that is happiness, p.5

6. The idea behind restorative justice stem from an age old religious tradition of justice and fair play where punishment, rehabilitation, and forgiveness involves not only the offender and the victim, but the community as well. (Bazemore and Schiff 2001: 117)

From My Cot, I Imagine

Tyrone F. Muhammad

Each day I awaken from a state of second death. Transfixed. Staring at the ceiling. Seeking confirmation of my subjugated reality. Drawing from awakened consciousness, sleep reveals an unpopular truth: the beauty of death. If death is as enjoyable as sleep, I welcome the possibility of eternal rest from this grim reality. Unfortunately, the forces of heaven still have need of my isolated shell. So eternal rest escapes me, and has escaped me for fourteen years.

I imagine my 3-foot wide prison cot as a 3-foot wide wooden plank aboard a merchant slave vessel. I imagine traveling several million square miles across the Atlantic Ocean, shackled hands and feet at the ship's bottom. Temperatures of 100 degrees and lava, with no movement in this 3-foot wide space. I imagine the treatment of those captive souls. I imagine the stench of soiled bodies as death permeates the air like a long-unkempt morgue with no refrigeration.

On my 3-foot wide prison cot, I imagine the cries of the dead: the agony, the pain as rats' nibble on month-old, untreated sores, with each nibble producing the feeling of being eaten alive. I imagine dying in a confined space with no human dignity, only to be thrown overboard as dark meat for the trailing sharks.

From 30 yards, I hear a familiar voice scream for the God of her people to deliver her from the clutches of savages finding joy in their ravaging. The voice of the woman given to me as a wife. How frightened she must be and how I lie, less than a man, helpless to defend the woman who has given me so much of herself. Over and over she screams out my name. With each scream, the God of my fathers grows void. My faith in the God of my fathers is no longer binding. So, I lie 3/5 or less on a 3-

foot wide plank, wishing and hoping this ship (prison) would sink.

My 6'1 frame lies motionless on my state-issued, 5 and 3/5-foot cot. I soon rise from my stupor after realizing my condition of isolation is nothing compared to the condition my ancestors were relegated to. My rise becomes more focused. My rise becomes more methodical. I now rise with a purpose to grow beyond my concrete and steel box. My purpose for rising now gives me the energy to overcome this prison industrial hell.

This plot is played out each day I awaken from second death. Prisoners must tap into their inner greatness to survive this unnatural condition: a condition that pushes against the very nature of the human will. The ancestral slave ship analogy is my way of finding strength, as well as downplaying the hell that has engulfed me for nearly two decades.

The very nature of prison engenders uncertainty. Prison wasn't designed to be a ship for healing. The way each prisoner navigates his unavoidable reality is the difference between peace and stress, life and death. For me to make sense out of the reality that is prison, I'm forced to engage my ancestral spirits. I figure, if they could overcome their dehumanization at the hands of man, then who am I to complain about my perceived inhumanity with the freedoms I still enjoy while enshrouded by concrete, steel, and barbed wire.

Dear Mother

Tyrone F. Muhammad

Dear Mother,

I write you from the enclosure of a 9' x 12' washroom (prison cell) that I sleep in and share with the child of another Mother. I write in the hope that my expression of love and remorse for my errant ways resonates in the minds and hearts of younger brothers and sisters who might be guided by my words. If I can touch one young person with my words it will be my drop of water into the ocean of humanity.

Mother, I want you to know that these days your instructions to me when I was a young boy ring louder than ever before. I remember the time you said to me, "I am your only friend, No one will love and protect you the way that I will, and when you get in trouble you will come to see who's really in your corner." Mother, in my immaturity I thought you were being a bit over-protective of your eldest child. My lack of understanding of the dangers awaiting me at every ghetto corner caused me to believe you were just trying to stop me from having fun with my friends. Oh, how I wished I had listened to your wise counsel. As you predicted, those friends I thought would be there for me during my hard trials of imprisonment are nowhere to be found. The way my friends have abandoned me, it is as if I never had any friends at all.

Mother, right now, while serving a 40-year prison sentence, your words to me are like a curse upon my mind. As an adult, I now perceive the truth of your desire to keep me out of harm's way. All you wanted for me—a black boy living in a hostile and violent ghetto—was to beat the odds of premature death or imprisonment by teaching me how to navigate in the war zone of Afghanistan Chicago. I must say. Momma, I beat death, despite living in a war zone. Unfortunately, I was unable to escape prison. Prison, though, is synonymous with being dead.

Mother, forgive me for dying on you. Now that I've destroyed 20 years of my life, my goal is to warn those kids out there about the horrors of prison. I will tell them that prison is an institution primarily built to destroy the young years of any boy or girl who believes it is possible to defy their parents and avoid becoming a victim of their own actions. I will tell them prisons aren't built for old people; once they get caught in the web of prison, escape is impossible.

Mother, I know you wonder in the sadness of your heart why we boys fall into such dreadful circumstances. You see. Mama, when we are young, our minds trick us into believing we can out-run time. We are unable to comprehend the fact that things must ultimately come to an end—even our folly. As young boys, time seems to have no end. Our ignorant disrespect of time is our Achilles heel. In serving prison time I now realize you were trying to protect me from the consequences of my inability to properly navigate the measure of time.

Mother, serving 14 of the 20 years I must serve of my sentence has allowed me to fully understand the importance of having a wonderful caring parent. My being inexperienced with the realities of life meant that I wouldn't adhere to the advice of a wise Mother. I'm sure other kids are experiencing the same problems I did. Now that I have children of my own, I can empathize with what you put up with in raising me. I guess it's normal for children to be so stubborn. But now that I am a man, I realize that is no excuse.

Mother, my stubbornness caused you and me excruciating pain. This type of pain heals over time but the pain of doing time away from you disturbs me the most. Mother, I want young people to know my isolation does not allow me to hold your hand for a simple walk in the park. If you get sick I am unable to provide you comfort. My separation from you keeps me shut off from the love a mother and son naturally share. Mother, the pain I feel in my chest for not being there for you is not fair. Is this pain only for the ghetto-fostered child, or can other children not raised in the ghetto relate to the hurt bursting through my soul?

Appendix -34

Mother, I can't make up for the time the judge sentenced me to, but I can make my time with you in the future greater than any time in the past. And with the strength of your love and DNA running through my veins I will one day depart the kennel of incarceration. On that day, my halo will wipe away all past pain. With my freedom. Mother, begins our new life. My Queen, I will never again disgrace the emerald crown of your heart.

Mother, please do not be ashamed of me any longer because I am on track to becoming the man you raised me to be. Time away from you has only increased my desire to love you harder than before. After serving 14 years out of your presence, Mother, no one and nothing will ever be able to separate our bond of affection again.

Mother, I love you!

Your Eldest Son,

Tyrone

My .22 Special

Tyrone F. Muhammad

Enthralled by the gangsterism celebrated on television from Al Capone to the Godfather. I was an impressionable kid who saw gangsters as heroes waging war against the evils of crooked cops. I viewed the police department as an institution of wicked white men who used their authority to keep black men under their feet, crushing our hopes of ever raising out of the poverty we affectionately called The Ghetto.

The police were the enemy of the hood-gangsters whom we all loved and admired. We loved the hood-gangsters because we perceived them to be men with authority who protected the community from outside elements. The hood gangster's ability to push against sweeping social, political, and economical injustices gave rise to their hero persona.

Every time the police abused their authority by harassing and frisking the hood-gangster it enhanced his street credibility. The tyrannical displays of them people (an expression that conveys an adverse difference between the hood and the police) produced in us a disdain for law enforcement. Those people couldn't be trusted because they lacked the compassion and understanding to grasp the plight of the hood-gangster who aimed merely to survive in an unjust environment that was and is regulated by bureaucracy. Furthermore, it didn't help that those people were often white men with no socio-emotional ties to the very communities they were assigned to police. At the end of the day, after harassing and locking up men from the community, creating even more dysfunction, them people returned to their plush communities as if nothing had ever taken place.

My uncle was one of the hood-gangsters I came to emulate. I thought the best way to achieve his gangster-like status was to somehow get my hand on a gun like the one that drew me to his holster.

My uncle was a person who enjoyed shooting guns. He possessed over forty of them. There was never a time when I'd see him without one. Because I looked up to him, I watched his every move. The bulge from his waist and his jacket created by the custom holsters he wore drew my complete attention, like an airplane in the sky attracts the attention of an earthbound toddler. Being a mannish thirteen years- old boy, it wasn't long before I followed my curiosity to the stash spot where he kept his guns.

One day, after cutting class, I arrived home around the time I thought everyone was either at work or running the streets. I soon found myself prying open my uncle's bedroom door with one of Grandma's butter knives retrieved from the kitchen drawer (I can't exactly remember where I picked up the idea to use a butter knife to open doors. Maybe I learned it from the television, or maybe I saw someone else do it when I was younger and the idea just stuck with me somehow.) After about five minutes of wiggling the butter knife back and forth between the door frame and door like a skilled thief, the sound of success surprised me as the door lock detached itself from the frame.

Upon entering my uncle's room, I began rambling through the obvious spots, starting with the dresser drawers. Being careful not to disrupt the contents of the drawers, each piece of clothing was handled as if holding the head of a newborn. Ten minutes into my search I discovered nothing, so I moved on to the closet, beginning with the floor. Making careful note to replace everything back just as I found it, I grew more frustrated with the opening of each box and the investigation of every bag. Beads of sweat trickled down my forehead. Since my uncle was a no-nonsense type of dude, I knew if he caught me rummaging through his things, a well-whipped ass was soon to follow.

My fear of my uncle catching me had me on edge. Every sound I heard frightened me; every car that pulled up near our house summoned my presence to the window. It's amazing I had the heart to carry out such a devious act. Having found no success on the closet floor, my attention shifted to the upper-shelves. At thirteen, I wasn't yet tall enough to reach the upper shelves, so I had to use the wooden school chair my uncle had at his desk as a makeshift ladder.

The makeshift ladder was one of the items stolen by my uncle when he was younger. According to the story my cousin told me, my uncle was then around the age of fifteen. It was said he and about five of his gang banger homies broke into a local grammar school with a stolen U-Haul truck and practically cleaned the whole school out of computers, typewriters, projectors, TVs, desk, chairs, and other classroom materials. I was also told that my uncle and his crew fenced the stolen material to a cat that owned a junkyard for five thousand dollars. The money from the stolen school equipment was used to purchase guns and drugs. This act of deviant behavior was said to be the only crime it took for him to start his criminal enterprise.

What's funny about this story is that no one was ever caught for the crime. I always wondered "Whom did the Chicago Police put in charge of the investigation?" They obviously were incompetent. Even at thirteen, I was smart enough to know that if you got a search warrant for all the local gang bangers' houses, you'd be able to uncover something linking individuals to the grammar school robbery. And to think, here I was standing on evidence of my uncle's deviance—evidence that could have landed him in prison for years. At the same time, the very chair from my uncle's criminal past was aiding me in my criminal activity against him. Some irony, huh?

Five minutes of lifting and raising the lids of shoe boxes recovered nothing. Too frustrated to move, I stood on the chair looking defeated and stupid. I thought to myself, "I know my uncle has guns in here. Where did he hide them?" As I pondered my next move, I recalled seeing my uncle fumbling with something under his bed. When I asked him what he was doing under his bed, he responded, "None of your business." He told me to get my bad ass out of his room. Replaying the day back in my mind, I instinctively threw myself under his bed like Detective Colombo (a favorite television character of my mother) and immediately started searching for clues that would lead me to my treasure.

More than five minutes elapsed as I slid under the bed, my new school clothes picking up every speck of dust and lint balls. The dirt on my clothes gave me an indication of how long it'd been since my uncle had last been underneath that bed. My adrenaline insulated me from the thought of my mother placing me on punishment for getting my clothes so dirty. My dirty clothes were the least of my problems compared to the beating I would endure if my uncle caught me under his bed. Such a beating would have received the approval of my mother once she was informed of my mannish activities.

I slid back and forth under the bed, hoping to discover any clue to help me in my search. I thought to check under the lining of the box spring mattress to make sure nothing was stashed in between. Nothing was found, so I flipped back on my stomach to continue searching on the floor.

Sweating and frustrated with my exploration, I noticed two of the 2 x 4 floorboards didn't have nails in them. I attempted to lift the boards, but the space between them was too tight for my fingers. About two minutes passed before I thought to use the butter knife that had gotten me into the room to begin with. Once the butter knife was inserted between the floorboards, I flexed it back and forth until one of the boards snapped open. Moving the 2 x 4 to the side, I put the butter knife down and used both my small hands to pull apart the second board and then I stuck my face in the space for a look. To my amazement, sitting on top of what seemed like black garbage bags were an assortment of black and chrome weaponry neatly arranged in space four to five feet in length and two feet in width. Everything from handguns to shotguns fitted snugly in place. Momentarily transfixed, my eyes danced upon the harmful sight as my nose took in the fumes of raw steel and gun oil.

Appendix -40

My uncle possessed an arsenal of weapons the Army would have been proud of, an arsenal that could get him sent to prison for the rest of his life. One by one, I pulled out every gun he had in the floor, carefully noting which side and in which order to place them back in. One by one, I examined each weapon like a trained marksman. I counted at least three shotguns, three sawed-off shotguns, two rifles (one with a small scope, one without), a machine-type gun with a banana clip (I didn't know it was a banana clip then, but I do now), and a host of handguns from .380s to .357s. But none caught my eye like the .22 special that would come to define my teenaged indiscretions.

I believed the .22 special was made especially for me. Why wouldn't it be, since it seemed to fit so snugly in my hand? At a length of five inches or so, it was designed to be concealed. What stood out the most about the .22 special was its sterling silver frame and the pearl inserts attached to the handle. When I got older, I'd learn that this style was the most expensive of all the .22 specials produced. For about twenty minutes, I fondled and caressed the weapon as if a virginal boy discerning the angles and curves of a woman's body. As I began to point it, shooting at the air, I felt like a giant, and from that moment forward, I knew my days of playing with toy cap guns were over. The hard part now was plotting how to remove the gun from my uncle's stash without him missing it.